RETRIEVER
PUPPY TRAINING
The Right Start For Hunting

Other books by Clarice Rutherford:

HOW TO RAISE A PUPPY YOU CAN LIVE WITH
Co-authored with Dr. David Neil.

RETRIEVER WORKING CERTIFICATE TRAINING
Co-authored with Barbara Branstad and Sandra
Whicker.

RETRIEVER
PUPPY TRAINING
The Right Start For Hunting

Clarice Rutherford and Cherylon Loveland

Alpine Publications Inc.

This book is available at special quantity discounts for breeders and for club promotions, premiums, or educational use. Write for details.

Printed in the United States of America.

Cover photo: Benchmark's Brio by Annette Smith.
Text photos: Sandra Whicker
Diagrams: Abigail Bridges

CONTENTS

Continued

ACKNOWLEDGEMENTS

*O*ur special thanks go to Sandy Whicker whose assistance in all aspects of this project were invaluable. Abigail Bridges gave generously of her time and expertise in reviewing the manuscript, Barbara Fleming aided with the early chapters and Mary Harding did her usual superb job of preparing the manuscript for publication. Bill Rutherford was always ready with a willing hand wherever it was needed.

We are very fortunate to have many good friends in the retriever world. They and their retrievers have helped us learn and grow over the years and made it all worthwhile.

ABOUT THE AUTHORS

A native Coloradoan, Cherylon Loveland has been training all breeds of retrievers for fifteen years. While associated with Duncan Labradors, she assisted in the training of competitive field trial dogs. She now has her own training kennel, Hunt-Field, and trains both hunting and field trial dogs.

Clarice Rutherford is co-author of *How to Raise a Puppy You Can Live With* and *Retriever Working Certificate Training.* A Labrador breeder and trainer for over sixteen years, she is active in numerous retriever clubs, breed and obedience clubs, has competed in breed, obedience, and field events, and currently teaches puppy classes at a Ft. Collins, Colorado, training center. Mrs. Rutherford obtained a B.S. degree in Animal Science and an M.S. in English from Colorado State University and was employed for several years at the CSU Animal Care Center. She currently devotes her time to writing and training.

Both authors agree that the tingle they get in their spine as they watch a retriever working out a difficult problem in the field is special—like no other feeling. It's what keeps retriever people working with their dogs regardless of weather, rough terrain, and long, hard days.

PREFACE

*P*uppies are not born knowing everything they will ever need to know. Many of the refinements required by their human leaders have to be learned, and some things are harder to learn than others. Each pup has his area of strengths as well as weaknesses. We believe that a good training program is one in which the pup and the handler can work through the weak areas of the pup's abilities and achieve success.

Puppies (adult dogs, too) learn best in a step-by-step progression. If a handler works on obedience commands one week, decides to begin hand signals the next week, doesn't train at all for two weeks and then decides to steady the dog to birds, he will have a very confused retriever whose performance will progressively get worse instead of better.

Many puppy owners have the desire and the ability to do a good job of training their hunting dog, but they lack a step-by-step program to use as a guide. When your pup has completed this program he will have the basic disciplines that are necessary for advanced training such as blind retrieves. He'll be ready to go when you put your hand over his head and say "Back." You will have worked out all the "Yes, but, Maybe, and I don't want to," excuses that all retrievers try to use.

This book is directed to owners of puppies in their first year, but the program is equally effective with young retrievers that start this program beyond that age. It gives your retriever the necessary disciplines and skills he will need if he is to become your reliable hunting companion.

Part I

Getting to Know Your Puppy

Am I ready for this . . . ?   Photo by Yosay

1

SELECTING A PUPPY

*T*he day your new retriever comes home is a great day! That bundle of energy has the potential of a great partnership for many years ahead. Therefore, it pays to spend some effort in locating litters and in selecting your puppy. If you haven't yet decided on a specific retriever breed, read as much as you can about the history as well as the current trends of each breed. Talk to different owners and breeders. Then decide which one seems right for you: Labrador, Golden, Chesapeake, Flat-Coated or Curly-Coated.

Various sources exist to help you locate litters of the breed you've chosen. Two excellent sources of breeders and litters currently available are *Retriever Field Trial News* and *Gun Dog Magazine.* You can also write to the American Kennel Club for names of retriever club secretaries in your area who can refer you to local breeders.

Many breeders are conscientious and raise puppies with great care. Take the time to find the right one and to ask a few basic questions about the litter. Reliable breeders will not only answer your questions but will be glad that you care enough to ask. In fact, your questions will help you to distinguish between caring breeders and those individuals who raise puppies only for what money they can get, caring nothing about either the quality of the breeding stock or the needs of the puppies.

You'll want to know if the parents are from hunting dog, field trial, or show stock (who can also be good hunters). Have the sire and dam themselves been used as hunting or trial dogs? Have either the sire or dam been proven (had previous litters that are now performing well)? Your puppy will not be a carbon copy of either parent but will likely have some behavioral characteristics of each. If either the bitch or the sire is inferior, lacking in retrieving desire and soundness, the puppies might be inferior. Retrieving ability and trainability are hereditary factors just like body type, coat, and type of head.

Equally important is information about the physical condition of the sire and dam. Ask about the parents' hips. If they have an OFA (Orthopedic Foundation for Animals) number, they are certified as being free from hip dysplasia. If they don't have an OFA number, have the hips been x-rayed and evaluated elsewhere? If so, by whom? Do the puppies' grandparents have OFA hips? Don't settle for anything less than verification of soundness; just because the parents run without limping is not a guarantee that hips are sound. Also check if there's any history of eye problems. Many retriever breeders periodically have their breeding stock checked to insure they are free of cataracts and other hereditary eye problems.

Healthy puppies in a clean environment get the best start.

OBSERVING THE LITTER

After you've located a litter, go see the puppies if possible. By six weeks of age you will notice differences in responses from the puppies; by seven weeks, the pups will be ready to leave their littermates. There may be only a few puppies for you to select from, depending on how many have already been sold and depending on which pick you have, second, third, etc. Some breeders reserve the right to do the selecting for each purchaser. This usually works out well because the breeder is trying to make the best match between puppy and person. Of course, when puppies are shipped, this is always the case.

The puppies should be in a clean, healthy environment. Does the mother look healthy? She might be thin from nursing, but she should be alert and friendly. If possible, see the sire, or at least photos of him. Are the pups being socialized? Listen to the breeder's comments. If the puppies are identified with ribbon collars or nail polish markings, the breeder has been observing the puppies daily and should have a good idea of the general personality of each pup.

Tell the breeder what type of puppy you like and then give special attention to the pups the breeder indicates would be right for you. If you are a strong willed person, you don't want the quiet pup in the litter no matter how cute he is. If you are an inexperienced trainer or an easygoing person, you definitely don't want the most aggressive pup in the litter.

OBSERVING PUPPIES INDIVIDUALLY

Carry the puppies you're interested in, one at a time, away from the litter, far enough so the pup can't see or hear his littermates.

Is the pup curious, tail wagging and exploring? Is he worried and trying to return to the litter? Can you attract his attention by clapping your hands, bending down close to him and having him run to you? Does he follow you when you walk past him? Even though you don't want a clinging puppy, you *do* want him to come to you at least once before he bounces away again.

Does the pup use his eyes? Does he watch a rolling ball or a moving object such as a rag on a string? Is he mouthy? For example, does he try to play with the moving object? Does he chew on your shoes? Grab at your fingers? A good retriever is a busy puppy, always doing something. At seven and eight weeks of age, will the pup pick up a dummy, will he drag it, or does he act as if he can't pick it up? These all indicate varying degrees of mouthiness and a general rule of thumb is that the mouthier the puppy, the more intense the retrieving desire.

Weather permitting, check out the puppy's water attitude. Walk into the pond with the pup; call him to you. Come out. Walk back in. Does the pup readily go in the second time? Will he go in and out of the water several times or does he sit and watch you go in and out of the water? Be sure it's a warm day and that the pup has easy access to the water.

Is the pup birdy? To find out, toss a dead pigeon in front of him. Does he sniff and mouth it with excitement— is his tail going 90 miles an hour?

Differences in behavior become more obvious as the pups play together.

Following indicates a willingness to follow leadership.

Pups should show no fear of water.

To determine the pup's degree of sensitivity, pinch either his ear or between his toes with your thumb and finger. Begin counting to ten when the pinch begins. If he reacts immediately before you get to one or two, the pup is overly sensitive; if he barely reacts by a count of eight, he's not sensitive at all, which often indicates a lack of ability to respond to training. How does the pup react when you release the pinch? Is he forgiving, licking you and assuring you it's okay, or does he turn his head away and ignore you? The latter pup will take longer to train and won't let you make many mistakes.

Play with the pups to compare degrees of birdiness.

Away from the others, does the pup pick up the bird and carry it?

Finally, realize that no pup is perfect. After you begin training, some personality traits will show up that you won't like. Training, however, is behavior modification and your training program will take your puppy's personality traits into consideration.

WHEN YOU CAN'T VISIT THE LITTER

You'll have to trust the breeder. Ask all the same questions initially, and ask about the observations you would make if you could see the litter. Tell the breeder the type of puppy you want, then rely on the breeder to make the final decision.

Many breeders require a deposit if you want a puppy held for you. The remaining payment is made at the time you pick up the puppy, or just before shipping. You should receive the puppy litter registration at this time, or the promise that it soon will be in the mail.

THE OLDER PUPPY

If you are considering a puppy that is twelve weeks or older, you need to get two assurances from the breeder. First, the puppy must have been taken out of his pen on a regular basis to experience different environments; otherwise, kennel shyness may develop. Second, the puppy must also have spent time alone with a person on a regular basis (for example, fifteen minutes a day, four days a week); if not, his socialization will be retarded and much time and effort will be necessary to bring the pup to a normal attitude toward people. If these two aspects have been taken care of by the breeder, in other words, if the puppy training has begun, you can do just fine by buying an older puppy.

MALE OR FEMALE

When looking at the pups in a litter, you might notice the females seem to be further ahead in performance.

Females are more mature until about ten weeks of age, then the males begin catching up. If you haven't made a decision about whether you want a male or female, review the characteristics of each. Both sexes make excellent working dogs in the field. A male might be a flashier worker, but many males will continually challenge for the dominant position with the trainer. Females are not as dominance-oriented and are consequently a little easier to train.

Females have heat cycles, unless spayed. On the other hand, males are constantly looking for a bitch in heat and some males are prone to inter-male aggression. Females leave brown spots on the lawn when they urinate; male urine kills shrubs and evergreens. Males also mark their territory wherever they go. Females are generally smaller, and males usually have a heavier, blockier head. A lot of hunters think a spayed female is the best hunting dog for them.

DON'T BRING HOME TWO

If two puppies are desired, wait until the first pup is five to six months old before bringing home the second. By this age the pup will have bonded to you and will be spending more time in his kennel area. He will also be starting his more formal field training. The problem with two littermates is that the initial bonding is to each other rather than you. If they have each other, neither pup will give you his full attention.

People who decide to get two puppies from the same litter often do so thinking this doubles their chances of getting one really good dog out of that particular breeding. In reality, they're guaranteeing that neither pup will be outstanding. Modern research in dog behavior indicates that puppy-human bonding is essential to superior dog performance. It's a very rare person who can induce bonding by more than one puppy at a time.

BEST AGE TO TAKE PUPPY HOME

The ideal age is seven weeks since a puppy bonds very quickly at this time. He's as receptive to human leadership as he'll ever be. Eight to ten weeks is also a good age but be mindful that this is a fear period. Any severe fear he experiences, such as extremely loud noises or being aggressively treated by children or adults, may be very deeply imbedded and difficult to overcome. On the other hand, you shouldn't baby the puppy. Let him live a normal rough-and-tumble puppy life—just beware of extreme conditions. Shipping is often done at this age, and while some pups might react negatively to the experience, the healthy puppy that is active and alert is probably better off being shipped to his new home at this age rather than spending another few weeks in a kennel.

2

YOUR PUPPY FROM
SEVEN TO SIXTEEN WEEKS

*D*uring this important stage of his life, your pup's attitudes toward people, toward learning, and toward his own sense of importance are being developed. The trainability of your pup is strongly affected by his experiences during his first four months.

It is at this time that bonding occurs. To insure that your pup will be responsive to you as well as to other people during the rest of his life, he must bond to a person at this age. Bonding, to the puppy, means he has someone to respect, trust, play with, and show him what he can and cannot do. He has someone who cares. To you, bonding means your pup will follow you around the house, and look to you for approval of his just being there. It means you'll have a pup that is ready for puppy training.

THE BONDING PROCESS

Letting the pup know, on a non-verbal level, that you respect his being a dog and you want his respect for you as a human is what the process is all about. All puppies bond, but the independent and dominant puppies usually take longer than others. With these challenging types of puppies, if the owner gets discouraged and backs off, the pup retreats into his own world, and it becomes a no-win situation for both.

Bonding is done by spending time with your pup with no other dog around—going for walks in the fields, calling your pup to you every so often. It's done by taking your pup with you whenever possible, and by having him in the house with you.

An excellent way to begin the bonding process is to tether your pup to you. This method is described in *How*

Tethering can be done anywhere around the house.

to be Your Dog's Best Friend by the Monks of New Skete, and taught by Job Michael Evans in his seminars. The first few days your pup is home with you, put him on a 6-foot leash tied around your waist. Do this for twenty minutes, twice a day if possible. If you have a 4-foot leash, tie it to your belt. The leash must be long enough for the pup to be able to sit or lie down but you don't want a cord so long that it lets him wander several feet away from you. As you go about your business around the house, don't give your pup any commands such as "Sit" or "Down." If he insists on jumping, give a quick downward jerk on the leash. Prohibit biting or chewing by a swift bump or a sharp "No." After three or four days your pup should be fairly well tuned in to you. At this point, he has begun a one-on-one relationship with you. This won't have a negative effect on his field work. You're establishing the foundation of the dog-human relationship from which you will build a training program.

This type of leash control can also be used in the evening when you're trying to relax and your pup is full of mischief, or when friends are visiting. Sit on the leash on a chair with just enough leash exposed so the pup can sit or lie down. What comes next is the hardest for most people to do: don't touch the pup. No toys, no sit or down commands, no petting. Don't praise when the pup finally lies down. The message you're giving your pup is that he can't be the center of attention all the time. If you don't weaken and pet your pup, you'll get a lot of mileage out of this procedure. You're building his respect for you.

At bedtime, for at least the first week or two, put the puppy in a crate next to your bed. When he begins to cry, lightly rap on the crate and give a command such as "Quiet." If the crying continues, rap harder, and repeat the command. Be prepared to lose some sleep the first night or two, depending on the personality of the pup; some respond immediately to the rap on the crate, while others take longer. Small puppies will need to go outdoors once during the night, maybe twice if you're not an early riser. If the pup wakes you up after sleeping for several hours, this is probably what he needs.

SEPARATION DISTRESS

Another important aspect of molding your pup's behavior during his first few weeks with you is to achieve a balance between being with your puppy and being able to leave him home alone. If your pup is suddenly left home alone after having had you there (for example, going back to work after being on vacation), he can experience a state of isolation that results in fear and panic. Suzanne Arguello, a behavior specialist at Colorado State University, has been researching the factors involved in separation anxiety of puppies. She states that teaching the pup it's okay to be alone should begin while the owner is at home. If the pup is to be left in a small room or the backyard while you're gone, put him there occasionally. Let him learn to be comfortable there by himself while you're at home but elsewhere in the house.

Separation distress, if not attended to, can develop into separation anxiety, expressed by frantic barking and destructiveness that in extreme cases involves furniture, or even walls and doors.

Begin with short separation periods of five minutes, gradually increasing the length of time. If he's barking when you're ready to return to him, wait until he has stopped (at least long enough to take a breath), then open the door and tell him you're back.

The manner in which you leave and return to your puppy is also a factor in how he perceives your absence. If you're emotional and feel guilty about leaving him, he'll sense this and will become nervous and upset. Practice your arrivals and departures at the same time you're conditioning him to your absence. When you leave him, don't be emotional. No petting or special fun games. Such handling followed immediately by separation can result in more intense separation distress. Keep your departure low key. Speak to your pup and tell him you're leaving, then leave. Use the same phrase every time you leave: for example, "Be a good dog; I'll be back." When you come home, greet your pup warmly (petting is okay) and go about your business. Later, when you have time, you can have a play period, take a walk, etc.

A pup should not be allowed free access to the house while you're gone. He should be kept in a small room, a crate, the yard, or a pen.

INTERACTION WITH OTHERS

The Older Dog

Some of you will have an older dog at home and the puppy can play with him as long as it isn't a never-ending affair. Remember, the bonding must be with *you* and not the older dog. If the two of them play constantly, or if the old dog lets the pup mistreat him, they should be separated most of the time for the next three months. A young puppy is also influenced by the behavior of the older dog, and will quickly learn his bad habits, such as barking and kennel- or fence-running.

Some older dogs like puppies; others have to be separated.

Young Children

Pups can't handle harshness or inconsistency. (Notice we said *harshness,* not firmness.) This is why the mixture of young children and puppies is often detrimental to the pup. A child will start playing, then the pup's claws or needle teeth make contact, or the pup jumps on the child who then

You can buy chain link kennels or make your own.

screams and starts beating on the puppy. The pup gets the message that he's invited to play, and then gets punished for doing so. He's learning that humans can't be trusted.

Your pup can be trained to stay off children by giving a vigorous scruff shake (see p. 24) when he first starts jumping. Children can be taught not to tease a puppy by isolating the child (or the puppy) in another room or outdoors for five minutes every time the child gets too excited.

HOUSETRAINING

From the owner's point of view, one of the most important disciplines the puppy will learn at this age is housetraining. As with all things, some learn more quickly than others. If you have one of the slower ones, your routine will have to be more rigid, which means it's up to you to see that the pup goes outdoors often, whether he acts like he needs to or not.

Steps to Take

- Designate a specific area in your yard and always take the puppy there.

- Praise the puppy when he relieves himself there.

- Use the phrase "exercise" (or any command you choose) whenever the puppy relieves himself. When he has learned this association, he'll often respond on command which is very helpful when traveling, etc.

- Put the puppy on a regular mealtime schedule, don't just leave a bowl of dry food out all day long.

- Take the puppy to his outdoor area after he eats, as soon as he wakes up, and after his play period.

- Don't expect a puppy to wait long periods between trips to his outdoor area. Some can wait a couple of hours—others can't. Sometimes a puppy will make a puddle in the house immediately after coming in from outdoors. This means he doesn't understand the reason for going outdoors. He only urinates when he gets the urge, and the urge didn't strike until he came in the house. When this happens, try and remove odors from the carpet. Many pups consider it all right to use the carpet once they smell it has already been used. Use either white vinegar diluted 4:1, or a pet stain remover from a pet supply store.

• If the puppy makes a mistake in the house, clean it up. Don't slap him or push his nose in it. Reprimand with your voice if you catch him making a puddle or a pile and take him outdoors.

• Keep your puppy in the same room with you. Don't let him wander around the house.

• At night, keep the pup in your bedroom in a crate. He'll let you know when he needs to go out.

• Each puppy has his own time schedule for being housetrained. Very few are completely trained by three months, while most are trained by six months of age.

TRAINING BEGINS NOW

At this age even a minimum of effort pays big dividends. Your puppy should learn to recognize his name, to have good house manners, to sit, to come, to have fun retrieving, and to play in the water.

Put a buckle collar on your pup as soon as you bring him home—the younger you do this, the quicker a pup accepts it. Clip on a lightweight leash for short periods of time. Follow him around with it. If the pup insists on chewing the leash, pop it out of his mouth with a "No." Talk to him in a happy voice, with an occasional pat, to let him know that staying close to you on a leash is an okay thing to do. As the pup grows older you can extend the length of time he's on-leash, and can take him for short walks.

What would seem an obvious responsibility on your part is teaching the pup his name, but we're occasionally surprised to see dogs six months and older that don't respond to their names. Start now. Use his name as an attention-getter, whenever you distract him from mischief, and whenever you bend down and call him to you. You'll know you're doing a good job when his head pops up the instant he hears his name.

The sit command is usually easy to teach. With puppies younger than ten weeks, it may take longer to get con-

Give the pup several sit commands a day.

sistent results, but it'll come. Hold your hand with a goody in it above the pup's nose. Say "Sit" while moving the treat back. As soon as he sits, say "Good dog" and give him the treat. Don't expect him to stay there, he's much too wiggly for that.

For the very young pups or those that are too bouncy to put their tails on the floor, quickly give a tidbit when the pup's hind legs bend even the slightest amount. You'll be amazed to see a good sit in two or three days. Continue using treats until a snappy sit is part of your pup's repertoire, and then you can gradually stop giving tidbits. Give your pup several sit commands a day, anywhere in the house, any time you think about it.

The here command is also started in the house, done randomly several times a day. Whenever you know you can get your pup's attention, bend down, clap your hands, and say "Rover, Here," (the command we will be using in our training program instead of "come"). The big advantage at this age is that all puppies love to run to their person. They'll even come to you outdoors at this age, but be sure you're close to the pup before you call him. You must always be successful.

Teaching Good House Manners

Earning your pup's respect now helps with later training. Teaching him to behave in the house is the way to get started. The pup arrives at your house having learned to respect his mother and having learned the hierarchy of his littermates. He now has a new pack to learn about and to discover where he fits. If you set certain standards of behavior and help the pup learn what he can and cannot do in the house, you're earning his respect. If you let him run wild, except for randomly shouting and occasionally beating him, you're telling him the pack leader position is up for grabs. If he accepts the position (and he will), it means he will do things his own way in his own sweet time. All young puppies must be taught how to behave around humans. The younger the pup, the easier and quicker he learns.

If your puppy arrives at your house at seven weeks of age, by twelve weeks the two of you should be in agreement about good manners. To accomplish this, the distraction technique works very well. It's a subtle type of training because it's simple and trauma-free. Nevertheless, your puppy is actually learning to behave the way you want him to around the house.

Pups are always ready for mischief.

Most puppies will try something such as pulling on a curtain or unraveling toilet paper, once or twice. If you distract them (make a noise, clap your hands, slap a table top, call loudly), and don't make a big fuss, they'll lose interest and forget about their mischief. Distraction has the added advantage of teaching the puppy to pay attention to you because you insist on it, if necessary by picking up the puppy. After the pup has been distracted, tell him he's a good dog and give him his chew toy. Distraction doesn't

Most pups understand the scruff shake if it's done vigorously.

work well with 4- and 5-month-old puppies but is very effective if started with 2-month-old pups. In contrast, the puppy that is constantly being screamed at, continually being chased and spanked, soon learns to tune out people. This can create a real problem puppy.

Save the strong discipline for the two or three behaviors that are absolutely forbidden in your home, such as chewing on electric cords or furniture, jumping on children, or getting on tables or counters. Scruff shaking is effective for most young puppies. Grasp the loose skin under his ears, at the neck, and give two or three vigorous shakes to the sides, looking him in the eye, then release. If you don't get any results from the scruff shake, you either didn't do it vigorously enough, or you have a very strong-willed puppy. If

Decide now if your pup will be allowed on the furniture.

this is the case, the scruff shake can be made more effective by quickly putting the pup on his side on the floor before shaking his scruff. (The element of surprise is part of the effectiveness.) This puts you in a very dominant position, and the stubborn puppy in a very submissive position.

Another method of strong discipline is to slap the under-jaw of the pup with your open palm in rapid succession (three or four slaps). This is sometimes effective when nothing else works. The use of these punishments presumes that you've caught the puppy in the act and that you're saying "No" along with the punishment.

Exploring the World

The training you give your young pup at home is only part of his education. An equally important segment of your pup's life is acquiring the confidence that comes from meeting other people, dogs, and things. It's natural for puppies to be startled or to shy away from something they've never seen before, or from someone who is loud and overwhelming. You can help your pup learn to deal with new experiences by going to the person or thing, and letting him sniff and approach at his own pace. Dragging him to whatever has frightened him will not help him overcome his fear.

When meeting other dogs or puppies, keep your pup on a loose leash, holding it high enough to prevent tangling around his legs. A tight leash makes a dog feel vulnerable and he'll react with either fear or aggression, either one of which can invite a fight. Let the dogs sniff around each other while you talk to your pup in low soothing tones. Usually, the two will either start to play, or will go on about their business.

Pups that train to be guide dogs for the blind spend much time experiencing the many sights and sounds of town life. The purpose of this training is to encourage a very confident temperament. This should be a goal for all dogs, and certainly is one of major importance in retriever training.

LEARNING TO RETRIEVE

Start short and keep it fun. For the 7- and 8-week-old puppy, use a knotted sock thrown 2 to 4 feet in front of the pup. Pat the floor and coax him to bring it back to you. If your pup runs away with his treasure, use a hallway or tie a cord to his collar to keep him from running off, while you coax him to you. When the pup is a little older, you can use a tennis ball and a puppy dummy.

If your pup is hesitant about picking up the sock, be patient. Praise him as soon as his mouth touches it, then throw it again, but not more than two or three times per session. The pup will quickly progress from mouthing to picking it up to carrying it.

If your young pup doesn't retrieve, don't worry. Pups mature at different levels. Some pups aren't interested, others need to learn to focus their attention. To create excitement, tie a white rag on a cord and let the pup chase it as you drag it around. Keep it just out of reach so he has a good

Use a hallway to encourage the return of a knotted sock.

A moving lure focuses a pup's attention on the chase.

chase before he catches it. Praise him, then take it out of his mouth.

Another game to focus attention and emphasize the return is the Old Tennis Ball on a String routine. Skewer two holes in the ball and run a cord through with a large darning needle. Use this as a game, not a retrieve. You can roll the ball in a circle at the end of its 8-foot cord, and then bring it toward you, letting the pup catch it. Or you can run backwards, keeping it in front of the pup and letting him catch it and bring it to you for praise.

Get the pup excited before throwing the dummy.

Teach your pup the fun of retrieving a dummy. Get him excited about it (a canvas puppy-size dummy) by teasing him with it right in front of his mouth and giving it a quick toss. Do this while sitting on the floor or the ground. Make it a game. Relax and enjoy yourself. When he loves to run and grab that dummy, start throwing it for him while you're taking walks in fields or open spaces. Keep the throws the distance he's comfortable with—some pups will be ready for long throws a lot sooner than other pups so don't rush it. This is still fun. Don't make him sit before you throw it and don't make him sit when he brings it back. If he drops it, pick it up; he'll learn the hold command soon enough. Take it on faith that expecting too much from a puppy at this age is going to mess up your retriever training program later.

Keep the pup running after the ball . . .

. . . until he brings it to you.

Introduce the pup to feathers at this age. Toss him a pigeon or a duck wing. Hopefully, either you or a friend is a hunter and can provide duck or goose wings. Some breeders keep a few in the freezer. Pigeons are often available through retriever club members, or are occassionally for sale in newspaper classified ads. Some pups do better retrieving a pigeon rather than a wing which they treat as a delightful toy for chewing.

Some puppies are ready for a little more formal retrieving by twelve to fourteen weeks of age. Hold your pup in a sitting position while a friend tosses a dummy about ten feet in front of the pup. Release the pup while the dummy is still in the air. This is described in Chapter 4. Give your pup no more than two or three of these retrieves at a time, but if he's ready for them he might as well get started.

Puppies should begin playing in the water if weather and water temperature permit. Keep it casual and fun, wading in with your pup. Remember that young pups are very sensitive, and no progress can be made in their water attitude if they become frightened by the antics of an over-zealous owner.

A pup can play with a dummy, but a retrieve shouldn't be expected.

SUMMING UP

You won't hurt your puppy's psyche by *guiding* his activities—teaching him the difference between yes and no. The dog belongs to a species that has never lived in isolation. In the wild, pups would learn their lessons from littermates and other members of the dog pack. You and your family now take the place (in the pup's genetic memory) of the litter and the pack. He needs that environment to develop normal dog behavior.

Early discipline of a puppy is a two-way channel. Both the pack leader and the puppy have their own responsibilities. Yours are greater, certainly more complex, because you're the leader and the architect of the program. Your pup's responsibilities are, nevertheless, of equal importance. He must respond to what pleases you, avoid what displeases you, and accept you as his new pack leader. This is part of the learning process that will continue the rest of his life.

3

PERSONALITY TRAITS

*E*very animal keeps a certain portion of himself to himself, but the more a puppy reveals of himself, the easier he is to train. Puppies reveal themselves when they are neither fearful nor constantly being challenged or confronted. One of the best ways to accomplish this optimum level of training is to take a thoughtful look at your pup's personality. Understanding his traits will enable you to adjust your training procedures to bring out the best in him.

Most retriever pups fit into one of three main groups. The first category includes the pups that are pliable, enthusiastic, happy, energetic, forgiving, and in general easy to train; the kind of puppy everybody wants, most people think they have, and few do. Some people get lucky and get one of these pups the first time around. They assume that all retrievers are this easy to train, then spend the rest of their lives looking for another pup that's as good as their first.

The second category of pups can be just as lively and lovable as those in the first category, but as they get past four months of age, and as they begin their training, certain personality traits begin to appear. They might worry, or sometimes be hesitant. They might be enthusiastic but only on their own terms. They might get a little uptight during training and lose their ability to concentrate. Such a pup has the potential for being a dandy working retriever, but your training procedures must deal with these problems. Some pups need more repetition to learn each command, some need lots of encouragement, others need a strict routine that doesn't vary. Most quirks can be worked out fairly easily while the puppy is young, but before you can work on these, you have to be objective about your puppy and continually read his behavior.

Then there are the dominant pups. They'll constantly challenge you for the pack leader position, and will resist doing what you ask of them. These pups need firmness and consistency and an owner who has an equally strong personality.

PERSONALITY TRAITS

When you begin to recognize specific traits in your puppy, you'll better understand his personality type. Training means you accept your pup as he is, and you *teach* him to be a good worker. A lot of a puppy's qualities can get better or worse, depending on the training he receives.

Willingness

The degree of willingness, or the desire to please, determines how easy your puppy's training will be. A pup that has a low level of willingness requires more repetition and more structure in the daily routine. Tractability is another word for this trait of the pup that comes when you call, bounces around you, and waits to see what you want to do next.

Curiosity

Curiosity is another very positive trait because it often indicates that the pup has a lack of fear. The pup is busy all the time ("What's over here?"), or he runs to a pile of rocks because he's never seen anything like that before. Curiosity is also an indication of the ability to concentrate on what he's doing at the moment.

(Photo credit: Annette Smith)

Distractability

Don't confuse curiosity with the opposite and negative trait of distractability. This pup is always trying to smell the butterflies, or a blade of grass, or a bush he's sure some other dog has marked. He's so busy moving from one detail to another that you can't get his attention. In retrieving, he'll run out to get the dummy you've thrown but then he'll proceed to chew on a stick or whatever else is there, smell a few blades of grass, and run happily back without the dummy. This pup will need to be taught how to concentrate—the trainer will need to be infinitely patient.

Energy

Energy is a trait that people usually have definite ideas about; some prefer the super-charged, others the calmer pup. The high-energy pup is a Type A ("Let's do something. It doesn't matter what!") High energy is a trait that makes for a stylish dog, but if combined with willfulness, the pup will require a lot of training. Many people seem to equate calmness with stupidity and high energy with ability. Perhaps a better way to evaluate the desirability of levels of energy for each individual trainer is to equate it with control or lack of control. How much of *your* energy must be spent in controlling your dog's energy? The ideal dog has plenty of energy and desire for retrieving and yet is calm enough when working to concentrate on you. The lethargic dog also requires a lot of energy; just keeping him moving is exhausting for the trainer.

If your pup isn't as flashy as you might wish, be careful to remain patient. Your training sessions should be involved with building your pup's confidence as well as his physical energy level. If this is done, his performance can readily develop into a working speed that will be very acceptable to you.

Sensitivity

It is difficult to work with both extremes of touch-sensitivity. The pup with a high tolerance for pain won't feel any pressure on his collar during leash training, nor on his ear during force-fetch training. If this trait is combined with willfulness or stubbornness, training becomes most difficult. In contrast, the pup with a very low pain tolerance (sometimes called "soft"), cringes, rolls over or runs away with even the lightest pressure on the collar during obedience training. The middle range pup responds to voice training as well as to reasonable collar pressure and force fetching, while still being tough enough to go through thick cover and cold water.The extreme in *sound* sensitivity is seen in the pup that is frightened by the noise of the vacuum sweeper or other household or street noises.

This is the age that retriever puppies don't have any training problems. (Photo credit: Jan Owen)

Willfulness

The willful pup is very independent ("I'll do it *my* way"); he will be on AM while his handler is on FM. Unyielding is another term for this trait. This pup might be more destructive in the house than the average puppy. Willfulness is sometimes considered to be the same as stubbornness, but actually the stubborn pup is more difficult to train. He plants himself and won't do anything, whereas the willful pup, given time and consistent training, can be convinced to work with you on *your* frequency.

Shyness

The shy puppy might cringe and stay away if you raise your voice. He might be fearful in new places, and won't approach other people. Training this pup to be a hunt-ing companion will take much time and calm firmness, and not all people have the patience for this.

If you feel sorry for this pup when he acts shy or frightened and you sympathize or pet him you are rewarding his behavior and encouraging him to act that way in the future. Instead, speak to him in a pleasant, firm voice but don't pet or tell him he's a good dog until his behavior is more what you want it to be, even if only for a split second. In training sessions, help the pup do what you want by using your voice and body movements to encourage enthusiasm. Keep his mind on you and off himself. Follow a few minutes of working with a short play period. Improvement will be slow but it will come.

The shy pup was born with a short supply of con-fidence and he will need a lot of patience. His behavior will gradually improve as he gains confidence in himself and in you.

SUMMING UP

The presence of negative qualities in a pup isn't necessarily bad.Some degree of these qualities are in every dog, and they can be corrected, but your training program will have to be tailored in accordance with whatever the degree of willfulness, stubbornness, high energy, distract-ability, or sensitivity the pup displays.

Watch out for labeling. If you have a pup that is willful and you train willfully, you'll constantly butt heads. You're insuring you'll end up with a willful dog. Take the positive qualities that are evident and build on those at the same time you show your pup that your will is longer-lasting than his. All pups have a combination of personality traits, any of which can be either encouraged or discouraged.

Part II

The Training Program

OUTLINE OF THE
TRAINING PROGRAM

PHASE 1

YARD WORK

- The "here" command.

- The "here" with a sit in front.
  Make eye contact with pup.

- The sit (stay).

- Here . . . sit . . . here . . . sit . . . etc.
  The pup remains sitting while you walk to the end
  of the leash and call him again.

- Here . . . pup comes to you and sits on command
  while you keep walking.

- Use a retrieve several times during the training session as a reward for good work, and to test his reaction to distraction.

FIELD WORK

Prior to Phase 1 retrieving is a fun game. Throw lots
of balls and dummys for the puppy.

41

- Puppy retrieves.
  - puppy sits on left side or right side if left-handed with long line on collar. Hold him in position and tell him to "Mark."
  - gunner stands a few feet to the side and throws dummy about ten feet in front of puppy.
  - handler releases puppy on his name while dummy is still in the air.
  - as soon as puppy picks up dummy, handler says, "Here," gives leash a pop if pup doesn't return immediately.
  - handler praises pup on his return, with or without dummy.

- Gunner gradually changes position and gradually increases the distance of the throw from the pup.

- The amount of "Hup-hups" by the gunner is determined by the puppy's attitude. Lots of noise if he needs help to become excited, no noise if he's already too excited.

- Steadying drill. Not to be done until the pup has learned the sit (stay) in yard work.

- Use birds once or twice, dummys the rest of the time.

PHASE 2

YARD WORK

- Obedience training.
  - Heeling.
  - The Finish. The pup learns to move from in front of you to sitting at your left side.
  - Heeling backwards. Use a wall, or fence, or vehicle to keep him from swinging away from you.
  - Pivoting. Teach the pup quarter turns, then teach him to stay against your leg while you pivot on your heel and he pivots on his rear.

- Applying Obedience Training.
  - Pup should sit before and after doors or gates open and should heel to the vehicle on-leash.
  - Pup should jump into his crate in the vehicle on command, should be given a sit command before he leaves his crate (so he doesn't bolt out), and a sit command as soon as he's out, so that he's under control.
  - Pup should learn the exercise command to urinate and defecate before he begins his field work.

FIELD WORK

- Marks become longer and can be thrown into light cover.
- Deal with problems as they arise.
  - Running to the gunner.
  - Helping the pup find the mark.
- The steadying drill is worked on continually.
- Work pup at his own level of progress. Don't be influenced by other pups in your training group.
- Water retrieves should be into open water, not on opposite banks, to prevent bank running.

PHASE 3

YARD WORK

- Force-fetch training.
  - The hold. Should be able to do obedience heeling while carrying dummy.
  - The fetch. From in front of mouth, halfway to the ground and off the ground.

— Fetching off the ground while walking past the dummy.

— Using tap of the stick while fetching dummy.

- Force to the pile.
  — Mark the pile for the pup before beginning to train. With pup at your side, throw a dummy to the pile for him to retrieve. Send on his name.
  — The pup sits in front facing the handler.
  — Pup fetches from pile of dummys three to four feet behind him when you raise your arm straight up and give fetch command.
  — Move pile six to eight feet behind pup and alternate back command with fetch command.

- The Slingshot
  — Always mark the pile before beginning to train.
  — With pup facing you, say, "Fetch," your helper snaps empty slingshot as soon as pup turns to go, repeat "Fetch."
  — When pup has no negative reactions to snap of slingshot, use a marble. Always say "Fetch" or "Back" before and after using a marble.
  — When pup has no negative reactions to a marble as he turns and leaves the line, marble halfway to the pile.
  — Always have your arm up in the back signal every time you say "Back."
  — When the pup has no negative response halfway to the pile, marble him as he gets to the pile.
  — Teach pup to leave the dummy alone when you drop it behind you after taking it from him.

- The pup now sits at your side for the slingshot routine.
  — Always mark the pile before you begin to train.

— Place your hand over his head and don't let him leave until you say "Back."

— Marble him when he leaves your side. "Back," marble, "Back."

— When he has no negative responses, begin to marble him halfway to the pile. When he has no negative responses halfway, marble him when he reaches the pile.

- Force to the Water.
  — Mark the pile before beginning to train.

  — Use a narrow piece of water because pup should be on a long-line to control his reentry into the water after taking a dummy from the pile.

  — Repeat all of the steps in the slingshot section. You and your pup will be close to the edge of the water for all of the steps.

FIELD WORK

- Use birds as well as dummys.
- Expect good line manners.
  — The pup should hold the bird or dummy until taken.

  — He should return to your side.

  — He should heel to and from the line on-leash.

- Continue extending the steadying drill from Phase 2 by adding birds and gunshots.
- Teach pup to mark birds rather than rely on the gunner.
  — Gunner can sit on ground after he throws birds.

  — He can lie down and be out of sight after throwing bird or dummy.

  — Gunner can walk to another place after he has thrown bird or dummy.

- Run Puppy on singles with either two or three gunners in the field.

- Use blanks in pistols and popper shells in shotguns.

- Have gunners shoot live birds as fliers. Pup will have to learn to mark these as they are different from using dead birds.

4

PHASE 1
GETTING STARTED

Your puppy has bonded to you; he knows the rules of the house; he's a happy retriever. He's fascinated with his world and demonstrates his readiness by going faster and getting busier every day. He's ready to move forward to new experiences.

The three phases of this training program take a total of three to four months if done on a regular schedule. Many pups begin the program around five months of age, some later, some a little earlier. The age depends on the pup's readiness: is he an eager retriever? Is he confident and outgoing?

The time to begin the program also depends on your schedule. Do you have a trip in the near future? If it's winter, with short days and snow, do you have the time and place to train? Puppies get teeth between four and five months. Since teething bothers some pups more than others, you may want to wait until your pup is past this stage before starting his training.

Once you begin, you don't want major gaps to occur in your training program. If you know you'll have a very busy schedule or a trip at a particular time, schedule the training program so you are between Phases 2 and 3 when this occurs. Then, when you're ready to resume training, a few day's review of Phase 2 will prepare you to begin Phase

3. But you can't keep waiting for the ideal time to begin because the older your pup gets the harder it will be to motivate yourself to find time to train an increasingly rambunctious dog.

EQUIPMENT

A 6-foot *leash,* either leather or web strap is fine; don't use chain leashes. Training can begin with either a buckle or chain *collar,* and for some pups we recommend a pinch collar. This collar looks a lot worse that it is. The prongs are not sharp; the effect is to apply pressure evenly around the neck. Many trainers think it is preferable to the choke-chain collar because it gives consistent control without constant heavy jerking. Use a medium size, lightweight pinch collar for puppies, and a heavyweight medium size for larger and older pups and adults. "Medium" refers to the size of the links. The length is adjusted by adding or removing links so the collar fits snuggly directly under the ears, not down on the neck. When using this collar, the leash is pulled, not snapped or jerked. When the pup responds correctly to the command, the pull is released.

To keep mouthing problems to a minimum, start the puppy on *canvas dummys.* Plastic dummys encourage a lot of mouth movement since puppies don't hold on to them very well. Therefore, it's preferable to save the plastic dummys for use after the force-fetch section of your training program. Don't put rope handles on the dummys, or if they have ropes, tape them to the dummy. It's too tempting for puppies to pick up the dummy by the rope, a practice that should be discouraged.

A *long-line* is a valuable tool in puppy training. You can buy one from a dog supply store or catalog, or you can make your own. Fifteen to twenty feet of braided nylon or webbing works well for this.

As your pup progresses in the training program, you will introduce him to *guns.* A starter pistol, or a .22 pistol firing blanks are sufficient for this. You don't need to use a pistol for every retrieve, just often enough to accustom him to the sound. When your pup becomes an experienced retriever, you can introduce him to a shotgun with popper shells, and of course, the final goal is using the shotgun with birds.

The *whistle* isn't used until toward the end of the training program, by which time the pup understands what you expect him to do. The whistle is used to remind him to pay attention, to hurry back to you if he dawdles on the way. If the whistle is used too much too soon, the pup ignores it, making it useless.

The *slingshot* and the *stick* (or horse crop) are used in the last phase of the program. They serve a specific purpose and the training program isn't complete or totally effective without their use.

Birds are seldom used prior to Phase 3 (the force-fetch). Dogs retrieve by instinct—the bird belongs to them. They'll run off with it, chew on it, and play games with it when you try and get them to bring it to you. Therefore, once you know your pup likes feathers, use dummys only, until you've taught him some commands and have some control over what he does. What about the puppy that loves birds but won't pick up a dummy? Use a ball, have fun, until the retrieve itself is the reward for the pup.

YARD WORK

Your training program will include both yard work and field work. Yard work is the term for the obedience and training drills portion of your program. Field work is the actual experience in working as a retriever, and gradually incorporates what is being learned in yard work to the field. It's a good idea to do yard work in the same place each time, and to move to different areas for field work where you can get together with friends or enlist the help of your family. In Phase 1, the field work is quite short and simple, ideally done after each yard session, and for convenience, in the same general area as the yard work if possible.

Training sessions should take place five days a week, for a duration of five minutes gradually increasing to fifteen minutes per session. If the weather is bad or the days are too short, train in your basement or garage. You must intro-duce your pup to a variety of environments at this age, but the yard work can be started in the home.

The Here Command

The importance of this drill belies its simplicity. Don't shortchange it. Take it on faith that it not only teaches the here command, but also rewards your dog for paying attention.

If your pup is not already leash trained, read Chapter 2 to get this done before you begin to teach the here com-mand. Your pup should be wearing a buckle collar.

With your pup on-leash, walk out briskly to the end of the leash. Say "Here," give a quick pop on the leash, then squat down (for the first day or two) and give the pup a treat when he gets to you. Repeat this exercise often, moving out briskly each time after the pup has come. The first few ses-sions will be short, five minutes for the pup of four months, a little longer for the older pup. Don't try to make him heel—it doesn't matter where the pup is walking at this point.

If your pup stays close to you, quickly walk off in the opposite direction. Sometimes you'll have to run, but keep changing *your* direction. Go in the opposite direction of your puppy, say "Here," give a treat, go opposite again, say "Here," treat or praise, and so on. After the first few days, begin giving treats at random, discontinuing the treats after about two weeks, and using "Good dog" praise thereafter.

The pup that has a desire to please will respond regu-larly after the first few "Here's," but continue a few more days because pups need a lot of repetition. The willful, stub-born, and high-energy puppies are a different story. The degree of their desire to please is completely overwhelmed by their desire to do their own thing. They will need some help to put things in perspective. We suggest you use a pinch collar with these pups. Available in pet supply stores, this collar does wonders for the overly rambunctious pup. As long as the pup responds to your commands, he'll feel no pressure from the collar. If he decides to go his own way, pull on the leash. When he does what you want, release the pressure.

Give the "Here" command.

Guide the pup to come to you.

Praise him as soon as he reaches you.

When you pull on the leash, the pup might slow down; he might even decide to lie down, not because of pain but because he can't do what *he* wants to do. The solution is another "Here" and pull. Otherwise, he learns that all he has to do to get out of training is to hit the deck. When your pup slows down, pick up your pace. The effect of the collar will surprise him and at first he might be vocal and resist, but as soon as he understands he has a choice, he becomes a happy worker.

The Dummy Toss

Retrieving rewards the puppy for good performance. In addition, he learns about dummy etiquette (no playing with it, no running off). After your pup has responded quickly to two or three "Here's" show him the dummy to get him excited, then toss it a few feet away. When you do so, he must go to it and come back quickly. Any form of playing with it should be discouraged. If he mouths it say, "Here," and pop the leash; get the pup back to you, with or without the dummy. Not until he is returning quickly, can you begin throwing farther than the leash length. The dummy is thrown several times during each session.

Another reason to include the retrieve in the yard work is to check out the pup's reaction to distraction. Some pups won't obey very well after they've retrieved the dummy but with repetition they soon learn to obey a command even after they've been distracted with the fun of retrieving. Some pups won't retrieve because of the pressure you're putting on them. It might seem like very little pressure to you but it's a lot to the puppy. Wait a day or two to try again because if you keep throwing dummys and he keeps not picking them up, that's what you're teaching. Throw a ball instead, or just play with him for a few seconds.

You can also use retrieving to get your pup alert and ready for training; throw a couple of fun dummys before you begin each session. If you have a high-energy pup, do some of your yard work before giving him a retrieve. Concentrate on controlling the energy during the obedience sessions. The more energy the dog has, the calmer and firmer the handler must be.

The Sit

When the pup is coming to you on verbal command with just an occasional pop on the leash, you're ready to add the sit. When the pup gets to you, place him in the sit position by pulling up on the leash, pushing down on the rear and saying "Sit." It doesn't matter where the pup sits, in front, or toward the side. You do want a *good* sit, however—no leaning, no lying over on one hip. The pup can be taught to correctly sit straight by using a light forward pull on the leash.

The pup should soon learn to sit without help from you, but until he does you can work on getting eye contact with him. Tap on his nose, even lift his head, or make noises—anything that will make him look at you. Let him know this is what you want because you're in charge of the training program and this will help him remember that fact. (Dominant personalities won't want to look at you and it might take a while to teach this.)

Help the pup to learn a correct sit. He'll soon do it himself.

The Sit-Stay

In retriever training, we don't use stay as a separate command. We teach the sit to mean "Sit there" until you're told to do something else. Diagram 1 illustrates the sit-stay concept which you can begin teaching when the pup shows you he understands the sit by sitting whenever and wherever you give the command.

Until now, after you've given your pup the sit command, you've either started walking again or thrown him a fun dummy. Now you'll be teaching him to stay sitting until you give him permission to move. The following procedure has proven successful in teaching the sit-stay.

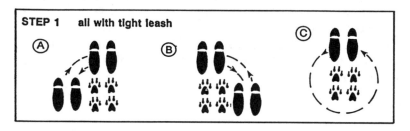

Step 2 repeats Step 1 but with a loose leash.

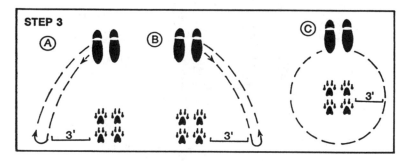

(1) With your pup sitting in front of you, fold the excess leash in your left hand and hold it taut, directly over the pup's head. Give a sit command, swing around to the right side of the pup and immediately back to the front again. Give a sit command, swing to the left side of the pup and back to the front again. Give a sit command and walk around the pup, returning to the front. Keep the leash taut

throughout this routine. If the pup moves at any time, give a pop straight up on the leash and repeat "Sit." Anticipate any movement—if the pup even moves his head, give a quick leash correction. If the pup moves out of the sit position, put him back.

(2) Repeat the movements described in (1), staying close to the pup, but lower your left arm so that the leash is loose rather than taut. Don't pause between (1) and (2), just lower your arm and keep going.

(3) Unfold the leash and repeat the same movements about three feet away from the pup.

(4) With your pup sitting in front of you, give the sit command and tug on the leash, lightly at first, gradually working up to a vigorous tug. You can put your foot on his chest as a brace, not a kick. Now you can tell him he's a good dog. Use praise throughout the exercise. After he is steady with tugs while you are a step away, move back to the end of the leash to be sure he's steady from that distance. Repeat this exercise daily for a week. Add distractions such as a glove, stones, or a stick thrown off to either side to test the pup's understanding of the sit.

Tug on the leash to help the pup understand that sit means stay.

When you back up to end of leash, your pup should sit until you give him a Here command.

The Here-Sit

Now that your pup has a good start on the sit-stay concept, you can add it to the here drill. This is the basis, the very beginning of the concepts your pup should understand before he can do a good job of learning the skills later that will make him a reliable hunting dog. People who short-change the basics of puppy training are the ones who wonder why their dog is out of control and isn't a good hunting companion even though he's been "trained."

The procedure is as follows: Give your pup a sit command—walk to the end of the leash—call him with a here command—give a sit command when he is in front of you—back up to the end of the leash. The pup continues to sit until you give him another here command.

This looks like a simple procedure but it can be very confusing to many pups. They have to sort out the sit-stay from the here command. It wasn't very long ago that they were sitting and running, sitting and running. Now they get a correction if they try to follow their trainer. Initially, your job will be to help the pup sort out these two commands, to teach him what you want him to do. You can say "Here—hup, hup, hup, with little tugs on the leash, encouraging your pup with your voice, then say "Sit."

If the pup moves out of the sit while you're backing away, use a leash correction at the same time you say "Sit." Timing is important—you want to catch him the instant he even twitches a muscle. To give a quick leash correction, hold the end of the leash in your right hand, have your left hand in front of you (you're facing the dog) with the leash going between the thumb and first finger. For a correction, your right hand pulls and your left hand goes up, which immediately pulls the leash on the pup's collar. If your pup isn't beginning to understand what you want after two or three days, go back to the sit-stay and train on that until the pup thoroughly understands and doesn't move an inch.

The next problem you're likely to have is a slow, hesitant pace on the here command, even a refusal to come to you. The pup is probably thinking, "You wanted a sit, you got a sit! I'm going to sit here forever." To overcome this situation, speed up your pace, jerk (or pull) when you say "Here." You can run forward for this, and turn toward your dog for the sit. After a few sessions of this, return to the more formal sit - here sit - here - sit routine, where you don't move until the pup has come and is sitting in front of you.

You will be using "good dog" praise to reward and encourage your pup. But too much praise will lose its effect. When your pup has been trying hard, he deserves it, but be sure he has earned it. For example, your pup has been having trouble but you get him through the routine and after a couple of corrections he does it right, so its "Good dog, good dog!" Throw a fun dummy so he understands that when he performs correctly he gets the reward of the retrieve and the praise that goes along with it. Then, it's back to work.

When your pup finally understands this procedure, it's time to teach him another refinement of the here-sit command. This time you will keep moving on the sit command, after giving your pup the sit command. A slight upward movement on the leash should help your dog understand that he is to sit even though you are still moving. The pace will slow down a little when you begin to teach this, but then speed up again as he begins to understand. As your pace increases, you might be doing a lot of forward jogging.

To encourage a brisk pace, run forward.

Help the pup with leash tugs if necessary.

Give the pup a sit command and move to the end of the leash.

When you get done, at the end of fifteen minutes, if you aren't breathing any faster than you were at the beginning, you're not working hard or fast enough. You should be huffing and puffing. This pace keeps you and your pup concentrating—learning to work with vigor. To put it another way, if you act like a dull, tired person, you'll have a dull, bored dog.

FIELD WORK

Retrieving with young puppies doesn't require much time or space and is fun, but a pup can easily learn bad habits. Field training that guides a pup to perform correctly without dampening his spirit is an essential part of puppy training.

We assume you've been playing with a ball and a puppy dummy and your pup thinks it's fun for you to throw these for him. In addition, by doing the yard work, the pup is learning to pick up the dummy and come straight back to you. Now it's time to have someone else throw the dummy. To insure that your pup will return to you, put the pup on a 15- to 20-foot long-line.

Sequence of the First Puppy Retrieves

(1) Gunner (thrower) stands several feet to one side of you. This encourages the pup to return to the "line," because that's where everyone is.

(2) Sit the pup on your left side with one hand on the collar, the other hand on the pup's rear, and say "Mark." This command alerts the pup that a dummy is coming and to get ready.

(3) Gunner gives a brief low key "Hup-hup" and throws the dummy about ten feet in front of the pup. With some pups too much shouting gets them too excited. Therefore, if the pup is already wiggling, the gunner should be silent.

(4) Release the pup when the dummy is in the air, before it hits the ground.

Holding the pup in this manner keeps him from wiggling.

(5) The instant the pup has his mouth on the dummy, say "Here." Pop the line if the pup doesn't respond. Don't wait. Don't let him push the dummy around and play with it. If he drops the dummy on the way back, that's okay, as long as he's returning to you. He'll soon learn to carry the dummy all the way.

(6) When he gets to you, praise him. Don't reach out to grab him, that only encourages him to avoid your hands. If the pup still has the dummy when he gets to you, scratch him behind the ear and praise before taking it out of his mouth. If he drops the dummy, just pick it up.

Don't give him a sit command. If you give too many commands before a puppy knows them well enough to apply them to different situations, you add an element of confusion that is difficult to undo, often resulting in a slow, worried retriever as he gets older. The retrieve in the field is a reward for the puppy, a release of pressure from the yard work.

Three or four retrieves is enough unless you have a high-energy pup. If your pup doesn't want to retrieve, don't panic. It's not uncommon for some pups to not retrieve on any given day. If he goes out to the dummy and touches it with his mouth, praise him the instant his mouth touches the dummy, and wait until tomorrow to try again. Instead of continuing with the retrieving, return home and play games with a ball. While at home, occasionally toss out a dummy with great excitement to see if his attitude has changed.

You can give your pup longer retrieves, and have the gunner move farther away from the line when your pup is returning with the dummy and not trying to run off. Because pups will naturally return to the closest person, *you* must be the closest person to the fall of the dummy. Diagram 2 illustrates this.

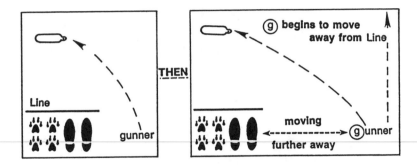

These first retrieves will be on bare ground or on lawn grass. When there are no problems with returns you can progress to cover, but use common sense. If the cover is too heavy and the throws too far, the pup will get discouraged.

Water retrieves are a game.

Water retrieves should start and finish at water's edge.

Try to get the pup to you before he drops the dummy.

Steadying

The steadying process is a gradual procedure during which your pup acquires the habit of not retrieving until sent. At this age, the goal is to teach him not to jump and twist around. This is a drill you can do after your pup is stable on the sit- stay.

Sit your puppy at your side and hold him by the collar. Leave your pup on a sit command and go ten to twenty feet in front of him. Look him right in the eye so he doesn't dare move. Silently toss the dummy a few feet off to the side and send him on his name when it hits the ground. When he picks up the dummy, move back to the line, calling him to you with "Here." Put him on a sit command again and repeat. If he breaks before you send him, try to get the dummy before he does, then take him back and try again. Gradually extend the length of time before you send him, and gradually extend the length of the throw. You can expand this exercise by keeping the pup on a sit until you get back to his side to send him.

Birds

Give your pup just a few birds at this age—maybe only for one or two days. This is difficult for many people since they think the more birds they throw for their pup, the better. There is, however, a good reason for withholding birds. Dogs retrieve by instinct (for themselves) and most puppies, sooner or later, will run away with a bird, chew on it, and play keep-away. His instinct is telling him that it's *his* bird. Therefore, until he thoroughly knows the here command, he should work only with canvas dummys. In addition, dummys will be his working tools throughout his training program. He needs to get acquainted and enthused about them.

The emphasis in field work at this level is on a happy attitude and on good returns. If you work on them at this point, you'll save yourself a lot of trouble later when it's time to work on other things.

5

PHASE 2
KEEP GOING

*A*re you wondering why it takes at least three months for this training program? It's because a lot of time is devoted to practice. A pup can appear to know commands very early in the training program. He's picking up on the many cues you unconsciously give him. But when distractions are introduced to the training session, or if you go to a different place to train, you will discover that you pup *doesn't* know the verbal commands. He hasn't practiced long enough for the commands to have moved from short-term memory to long-term memory.

A trainer decides for himself the quality of performance he wants from his dog. If you require a performance that is the best your dog can manage, you'll train until you get it. This requires working out any little problems that arise each day—using your leash and your voice for communication, back-tracking if necessary, and ending each sesion with success. It involves a brisk pace during the session, praise for good work, and enough days working together for the pup to become a consistently happy worker.

Observe your own training with the sharp eye you use when you watch someone else's pup. Does your pup respond to your "Here" with very few leash pulls? Does he sit quickly, with no leash correction and no second command? Does he remain sitting while you keep walking? Is he paying attenion to you during the session? Does he obey your commands as quickly after he retrieves a dummy as before? If he's a quiet pup, have you increased his enthusiasm? If he's a high-energy pup have you moderated his pace? If he's independent or dominant, are you getting his respect? This all takes time. When you feel your pup is performing the Phase 1 exercises up to your expectations, proceed to Phase 2.

YARD WORK

Heeling and Sitting at Your Side

When the here is very consistent and the pup is sitting solidly while you keep moving, you're ready to begin heeling with the pup at your side.

With your pup sitting at your left side, fold the leash in your right hand, leaving only enough slack to let your dog move comfortably at your side. Give the heel command and step out briskly. If your pup moves away from your side a few inches (he shouldn't have enough leash to get any further away), give the leash a sharp pop (or a pull if he's on a pinch collar) followed by the heel command. If you give the correction vigorously, he'll be back at your side and the leash will be loose, at which time give a brief but pleasant "Good" so he can learn that's where you want him to be. If he continues forging, do abrupt about-turns, which should be vigorous enough to surprise him and bring him quickly to your side. Give a second heel command when you about-turn. The turn itself is also a correction for not being at your side.

Expect a quick sit at your side when you halt. Your pup knows the sit command so an upward tug on the leash is sufficient if he hesitates. Apply pressure just in front of his hind legs with your thumb and fingers if he needs additional help. After a few of these to show him what you want, he should sit straight with no leaning on you and no sitting on one hip.

Some pups lag when they first start heeling. Others will forge ahead.

This pup is in correct heel position.

A Heeling Pattern

Using a 20- to 30-square foot area for the heeling routine helps keep the pace fast and allows you to use a variety of commands in a relatively short time. Both of these factors are necessary to maintain your dog's concentration and enthusiasm during the sessions.

Use dummys for corner markers. Since the pup might try to pick up a dummy, watch for this. If your command was "Heel" and the pup dives for a dummy, give another "Heel," jerking or pulling him to your side as you begin walking. If your last command was "Sit," do the same. If he gets to the dummy, say "No," put the dummy back and continue heeling or sitting.

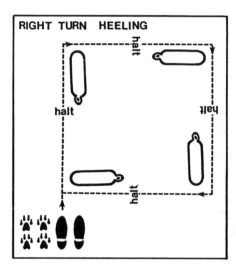
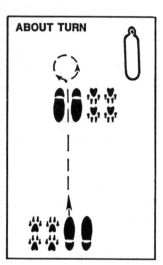

The dummys are the corner posts of the heeling area.

When you first use this heeling pattern in training, heel in one direction with a halt in the middle of each side, do an about-turn and repeat. Select from the following list what you will do each session, and when the pup is familiar with all the exercises, mix them up for a few minutes of vigorous heeling (insisting on heel position and quick sits). Throw a couple of fun dummys when you're finished.

1. Right turns, left turns; turns should be sharp.
2. About turns, U turns (turn into your dog).
3. Figure 8.
4. Oval, around 2 posts.
5. Circle a dummy.
6. Change pace; speed up or slow down.
7. Quick sits; several halts in close succession.

Regardless of your pup's personality type, all he needs to know is that he's under command and he's working with you. Beyond this, it's up to you to keep him busy—keep him

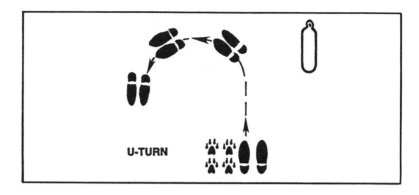

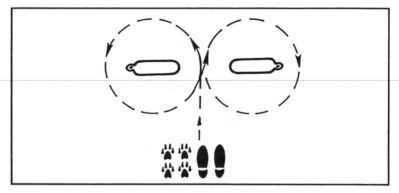

The figure 8 and the U-turn teach the pup to stay at your side regardless of turns and circles.

from being bored while he's learning. You do this by mixing up your training commands so he doesn't know what's coming next, and by praising (quickly and quietly so it doesn't break his concentration) when he's been working hard and doing well.

The Finish

Now is the time to teach your pup to return to heel position from a sit in front of you. You will use this later in his field work. After he has learned to hold the bird, you want him to return to your side when he brings it back to you. To teach this, put your pup on a sit in front of you; give the heel command, stepping back with your left leg. Guide him with the leash to make a circle to your left and then take a step forward which should bring him into heel position with a sit at your side. Gradually stop helping him with the leash and with your leg movements as he learns the command.

Heeling Backwards

This is difficult for both handler and pup because the pup will be going every which way at first. He'll try to walk

Use the side of a pick-up to teach the pup to heel backwards. A stick helps to guide him.

in front of you, then he'll try to back out behind you. This is an excellent time to start using your stick as a guide. Start with him next to a wall or fence. Say "Heel" and move backwards. If he moves out ahead, tap him on the front; if he scoots behind, tap him on the rear (if the stick is in your right hand, reach around behind you for this). Use the stick to guide his movements, *not* to punish him. When the pup begins to understand the backwards heeling, you can practice without a wall. This command is valuable in field work where you want to change position quickly and quietly.

Pivoting

Another heel concept helpful in field work is having your dog move with you to change the angle of his field of vision. First, teach quarter turns, both left and right. The sequence is: heel . . . make a quarter turn . . . sit. The pup will be on a short leash at your side so you can control his movements. Do four turns right, then four turns left, then praise. When your pup understands the turns, you can work on pivoting with him. To do this, your feet stay in place and you turn on your heel.

Applying the Sit and Heel

Don't get in a situation where you have to chase your dog through the neighbor's yard in the process of putting him in your vehicle to go training. Because he loves to go, he'll be very excited but must learn control. Give him a sit command before you let him out of his kennel (or the yard or the house, etc.). Then, open the door or gate, and give another sit command. Put on the leash and insist that he heel to the vehicle. When you're ready to start your field work, say "Sit" before you open the door of the crate (so he doesn't come leaping out), then open the door, say his name quietly, followed by "Sit" the instant he hits the ground. Put on the leash. When you've finished his retrieving work, he should heel back to the vehicle, sit, and then jump into his crate when you say his name. Don't take off his leash until he's in the crate. You might have to help him jump in at first by lifting his rear, or throwing a goody or a dummy into the crate.

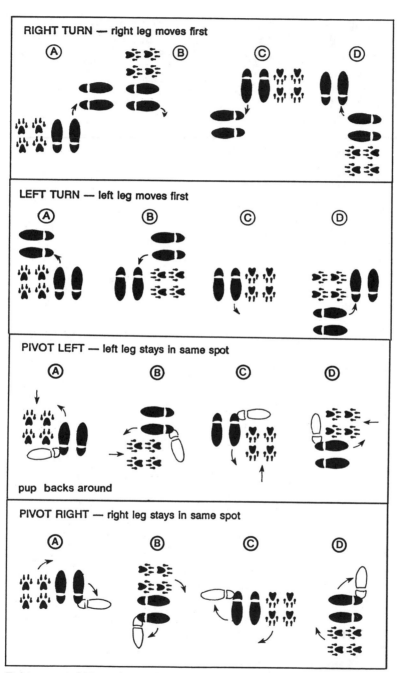

Taking an additional step for the right and left turns helps the pup to understand what he's doing.

The Exercise Command

When the pup first gets out of his crate for training, give him a couple of minutes to urinate and defecate. Use the same command every time. We use "Exercise." Some people say, "Hie on," or "Be a good dog." It doesn't matter what you say as long as it's always the same. When he does something, praise him, or if he doesn't need to do anything, call him with a "Here" and get ready to train. Don't let him run off any distance. Keep the pup on a leash, if necessary, until he learns not to run off. Whenever and wherever you see him do his business say "Exercise" so that he learns to associate this command with that action. As he grows older, he'll know to "exercise" quickly, and be ready to retrieve.

A pup on a sit command is always under control.

FIELD WORK

When your puppy consistently returns to you with the dummy, the gunner can move out into the field, as outlined in the sequence of first puppy retrieves in chapter 4. Hold the pup by the collar as he sits at your side. Release him on his name as soon as the dummy hits the ground and call him back to you with a here command as soon as he picks up the dummy.

Don't insist on formal sits yet when he returns, just let him run up to you with the dummy. Remember, don't grab for the dummy as this encourages the pup to run off. If the pup drops the dummy at your feet, simply pick it up and get ready for the next mark. The pup will learn all of these line manners in Phase 3.

Always holding the pup's collar teaches him to sit quietly until he's released.

The Marking Pattern

Because dummys thrown into light cover are excellent for building confidence, the marking pattern is a very good drill. Your pup should be an enthusiastic retriever before you start using this pattern.

The first throw should be approximately twenty yards out from the pup, thrown either straight in front of the gunner, or angled slightly back. If the pup successfully retrieves that one, the gunner should move in a semicircle for a total of three or four marks, continuing to throw them in the same direction. This not only helps the dog learn to hunt in front of the gunner but also prevents the confusion that will result at this stage of training if a gunner throws dummys on both his left and right side.

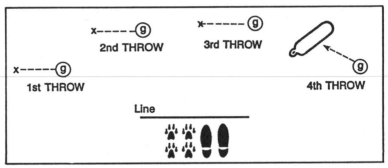

The distance of the gunner in the marking pattern depends on the ability of the puppy.

The pups that are doing well at marking the fall of the dummys in the Marking Pattern are ready to begin retrieving in more difficult cover. Any ditches introduced should be clearly visible to the pup and should be close to the line, rather than close to the dummy. If the cover is heavy, throw the dummy in an open spot within the cover so it's visible as soon as the pup gets there. If the pup keeps running around instead of staying and hunting for the dummy, "salt" the area. This means that you will place four or five dummys in the area where the mark will be thrown so he'll find one of them as he goes to the area. To teach your pup a long, difficult single retrieve, first run it as two or three individual singles, starting with the two of you close to the mark, and moving back toward the original line. Use white dummies, preferably canvas, but plastic will do if you are having no mouthing problems with them.

Running to the Gunner

Sooner or later, your pup will probably run to the gunner when he can't find his dummy. If this happens, the gunner should just stand there (the supply of dummys should either be in a bucket or otherwise concealed to prevent the pup from being rewarded by finding a dummy at the gunner's feet). In the meantime, the handler can walk out wide of the dummy and call the pup so he might see it as he comes, or the handler can say, "Hup, hup, hunt it up" (the pup will learn what this means), or the handler can throw a dummy which the pup will pick up and bring to him. The point is to try to keep the pup moving in the area of the fall until he stumbles on the dummy. You can't give direction commands at this level of training.

Helping the Pup Find the Mark

When the pup is running wide, the gunner can throw another dummy toward where the original dummy landed. Make sure it is thrown when the pup isn't looking so he doesn't associate the gunner as helping, then when it's in the air, he yells so the pup turns and sees the dummy before it hits the ground. This is preferable to having the gunner walk to the dummy and show the pup where it is because some pups quickly learn to expect help from the gunner and will even stop and wait for it.

Be sure to discuss your tactics with the gunner before he goes to the field to throw. When a situation arises where your pup needs help, it's very frustrating to try and instruct the gunner at that time. Make sure that person knows how to handle such problems.

A Drill for Steadying

In Chapter 4, the steadying drill was done with just you and your pup. Now you're ready to add the gunner. Ask him to stand about twenty yards in front of you and your pup. Give the sit command which by this time should mean to him: "Don't move until you get another command." Signal the gunner. He will silently toss a dummy three to four feet away from him. If the pup sits until the dummy hits the ground, send him on his name. There should be no straining on the collar (a buckle collar works best for this as you can get your hand under it for a stable hold). If you intend to use the electric collar after this basic training program, use a dummy collar for yard and field work. If the pup moves, even a little bit, the gunner picks up the dummy, returns to his position and throws it again. After the pup sits quietly and has retrieved several dummys at the distance of a throw of a few feet, gradually increase the length of the throw. The longer and therefore higher the throw, the more exciting it is to the pup. This drill will take several sessions, until the pup understands he doesn't get to retrieve the dummy unless he waits for his handler's verbal signal.

When the pup is steady, the gunner can move farther back for a longer retrieve. If at this distance, the pup begins to wiggle and lunge, the thrower should return to the distance where the pup was successful, throw a few marks, and then move farther away again. These are still silent throws.

This drill can be used continually throughout the rest of the training program. The gunner can add "Hey, hey," then a pistol and finally, a popper gun. The handler can occasionally release his hold on the collar. If the pup breaks, he can't be allowed to get the reward of the dummy. The gunner must get to it before the pup. Don't be in a hurry to release your hold on the collar. A puppy needs a multitude of repetitions before he completely learns a lesson.

Water

Water marks are thrown out in front of the pup who is sitting close to the edge of the water. The dummy shouldn't be thrown across onto the opposite bank, or even close to it, because once the pup gets out of the water, he won't swim back. He'll run back and forth on the other side without re-entering the water, or he will run all the way around the pond. This habit, once started, is very difficult to break. The problem with running the bank in hunting and field trials is that the cover might be so thick the dog has a problem getting through with the bird. It also completely blows his concentration, so that if two birds went down, he'll have no memory of the second bird by the time he gets back. Water retrieves at this age are to encourage confidence with swimming and returning with a dummy. If your pup swims with a dog-paddle, he should outgrow it with age and experience.

Training in Groups

Part of the fun of retriever training is working with friends who have the same interest. Ironically, though, while being around other people and dogs is good and necessary for your pup, it can also be detrimental. It depends on you.

When working with other people and their dogs, try not to compete with them. Strive for you and your pup working as a team, both doing your best. Any young dog will occasionally have an off day and look like a dud, or one pup might be progressing more slowly than another pup of the same age. Training requires a lot of objectivity on your part. Gear your training to *your* pup's personality and development on that particular day. Save your competitive attitude for an appropriate time.

SOLVING TRAINING PROBLEMS

If you have a problem you can't seem to overcome, don't waste time. A wrong behavior reinforced more than a few times can take months to correct. It's very difficult in a book to cover all aspects of the interaction between the handler and the pup, so go to someone who has had a lot of experience with retriever training and whose opinion you respect. Hopefully, that person will be able to objectively evaluate you and your pup and arrive at a possible solution for your problem.

Some owners have a philosophy that they will work with a pup the best they can, addressing his individual needs, until the pup is eight to twelve months old. If, at that time, training is more frustrating than pleasurable, they will retire this pup to pet status, finding another more appropriate niche for him. In the meantime, each pup deserves every opportunity to develop to his potential.

6

PHASE 3
THE BIG FINISH

*F*orce training, the final phase of basic training, forms your pup's attitude toward working for you. If you follow through the entire program, the end result will be a dog that waits for commands, intensely wants to go get that dummy or bird, and is ready to learn blind retrieves.

The ear pinch is a tool that forces the dog to do something he's already been taught. By the time you have taught him to hold, and to open his mouth on "Fetch," you will use the ear pinch to force him to do those commands. The stick and the slingshot are used to condition the dog to pressure. These tools, the ear pinch, the stick, and the slingshot, make your dog dependable when something arises that he doesn't want to do. They help the pup become more focused on what he's doing. He won't be so distracted by other things and will become a very eager worker.

The first fundamental of force training is a sense of timing. The pace of the drills must be brisk. If you take too much time between fetches, your pup will lose his concentration. Give your commands quickly and keep the pace moving.

Another aspect of training is developing a sense of knowing when to simplify or back up a little to an earlier level of training. If you hit a stubborn snag, for example, in taking the dummy off the ground, go back to a fetch that's easy for your dog, then move ahead again to the fetch that's been giving him trouble. Be sure your pup is comfortable with each step before moving to the next. There's no hurry.

By this time your training sessions will last about fifteen minutes. Remember the importance of ending each session with success.

YARD WORK

To enhance your pup's positive attitude toward retrieving, throw three or four fun dummys before each training session. The throws can be short. There's no reason to wear him out before he starts. Also, use the "Good dog" phrase occasionally throughout the session—he needs to know when he's doing good work. If he seems to be getting tired or nervous, throw a fun dummy to relax him.

The Hold

Even though we are teaching the hold command, we *say* "Fetch" every time we put the dummy in the pup's mouth for the hold. By the time we're ready to teach the fetch, he is beginning to associate the command with opening his mouth.

The first couple of days of teaching the hold can be difficult since a lot of dogs don't like to sit still while someone puts something in their mouth and then holds their mouth closed. Start with a wooden dumbbell or dowel or piece of broom handle, which aren't as thick as a dummy. In two or three days, switch over to a dummy.

With your pup sitting at your side, stand on the leash. If he doesn't remain in a sit when you put the dowel in his mouth, work on the sit until he's under control.

With your left hand on top of his head and your right hand holding the dowel in front of his teeth, say "Fetch" and immediately *put* the dowel in his mouth. (Don't wait to see if he'll open his mouth.) Then say "Hold," keeping one hand on top of his muzzle and the other hand under his chin. Start by having him hold for only two or three seconds; gradually increase the time as the pup becomes more comfortable with the procedure. Begin using a dummy during the process of increasing the time of the hold. Progress from holding the mouth shut to tapping under the chin. You can also put a finger in the V-shaped bone under the chin to keep his mouth closed. After a few seconds, use the drop command and either open the mouth to take out the dummy, or let it fall out into your hand.

You can begin with either a dowel or a dummy.

With one hand on his head, a finger under the chin helps the pup learn to hold.

As soon as the pup is holding fairly reasonably, start walking with him as he holds—you needn't use the heel command, just start walking. With one hand on his head, the other hand firmly under his chin, take just a couple of steps, then say "Sit . . . drop," and repeat the procedure. At first it's difficult for a dog to walk and then to sit while still holding—it's up to you to make sure the dummy stays in his mouth. Some dogs will stiffen up and be unable to move. In this case, talk quietly and coax him into moving. If he spits out the dummy, put it back in, say "Hold" and tap under the chin. (Be sure the lips aren't between his teeth and the dummy, which can be painful.)

The end result of the hold training is that you should be able to do any of the obedience exercises with the pup holding the dummy in his mouth. Also, the pup should be holding firmly enough for the dummy to stay in his mouth even if it bumps your leg. If your pup has a really soft mouth, tap the dummy with a finger to test the hold before starting to walk.

Help the pup hold the dummy when he first starts to walk.

Tapping the dummy encourages the pup to hold firmly.

The Fetch

By the time you're ready to teach the fetch, your pup may be automatically opening his mouth as soon as he hears you say "Fetch." To reinforce this reaction—so he will pick up a dummy (or bird) no matter what mood he's in, and no matter where it may be—you will use the ear pinch.

To begin, have the pup sitting at your side. Hold the ear closest to you and pull forward toward the dummy that is right in front of his mouth as you say "Fetch." If your pup won't open his mouth, apply pressure to the ear with your finger and thumb. Release the pressure immediately as soon as his mouth opens and you put the dummy in. Timing is what makes the method successful. The release of the ear pressure is the reward for taking the dummy. If the dog feels ear pressure after the dummy is in his mouth, he loses incentive and becomes confused. The sequence is for you to say, "Fetch . . . hold . . . drop."

Apply pressure to pup's ear until his mouth opens. Then release immediately.

To control head movement, position your hand through the collar. You probably won't need to pinch every time, and the degree of the pinch will vary. If the dog is slow about opening his mouth, he needs a hard pinch. Also, different parts of a dog's ear will be more sensitive than others; sometimes it's the tip, sometimes in the middle, sometimes down farther. Use the ear on the other side if the pup turns toward you and tries to "fetch" your hand. This also gives you a little more control over head movement.

Once the dummy is in front of his nose, if the pup turns his head, don't move the dummy. Pinch hard on the ear. A few of these will convince him that he can't avoid the fetch command. If he's stubborn, give him something to think about. When he turns to the right, keep the dummy toward the left. If he looks down, hold the dummy a little above his head.

Once the dog is opening his mouth and fetching consistently from in front of his mouth, move the dummy half-way between his head and the ground. Keep it close to him so he only needs to drop his head to get it. Keep your hand under the collar to help him raise his head once he has put his mouth on the dummy. (Some pups forget what they're doing down there.)

The hardest part of the force-fetch procedure is the fetch off the ground. Many dogs seem to have an aversion to taking a dummy that's lying flat so begin by putting the dummy on the top of your foot, or step on one end which raises its opposite end. When the dummy is finally put flat on the ground and the pup is still having a difficult time, lift it slightly to help him discover that indeed it can be done.

The speed of all these fetches should be quick. The longer the pup sits there, with you holding the dummy in front of his mouth, the more you're going to guarantee that he won't fetch. Occasionally, however, you will do this (hold the dummy a few seconds before you say "Fetch") to check whether he's responding to your voice command or merely grabbing the dummy because it's there. But at first don't do too much testing of this type.

The pup shouldn't move; he should just bend his head.

At some point your pup will clamp down on the dummy and not respond to your command to drop it. Simply pry open the mouth; don't get too concerned at this stage of the program.

When the pup is fetching off the ground, throw the dummy a couple of feet out so he has to move to reach it. If he wants to sit immediately after picking it up, heel him a few steps. If he wants to pick it up and keep going, tell him to sit. Let him know he's still under your control, that he's doing what *you* want.

Throw the dummy a few feet farther. Point to the dummy as you approach it and say "Fetch." Of course, you shouldn't point at it each time or the pup will fetch only when you point instead of on the fetch command. It's equally important not to let the pup anticipate the fetch command. He must perform on voice command only, not when he thinks he's close enough to lunge for it.

Your pup might have difficulty with always being on your left side as you point with your right hand. Some can't fetch when the dummy is on the other side. To prevent this problem, have your dog sit facing you. Tell him to fetch a few on your right side, pointing with your right hand, and on your left side pointing with your left hand, and then do a few with no pointing. This variation should correct or prevent the problem. If it doesn't, throw fun dummys to relax him, then tell him to sit and try again.

At this point you can start using your stick or horse crop to teach the dog to fetch under adverse situations. It is not used as a punishment; it will help condition the dog to pressure. With many dogs, a light tap isn't even going to be felt, but he will learn to fetch even though he's being distracted. Even a hard tap isn't going to be painful, but the dog perceives it as more pressure. Your pup will learn that when you say "Fetch" there should be no excuses for not doing so.

With the dog sitting at your side, hold the leash and stick in your left hand. Put the dummy in front of his mouth, say "Fetch," a couple of times, then tap him (barely touching) with the stick on his hindquarters. He's still sitting— all he has to do is open his mouth when you say "Fetch." Move the dummy forward a few inches so he has to reach

Don't let the pup dive for the dummy until you say "Fetch."

Give the pup a fetch command as you pass a dummy. Don't slow down.

If the pup doesn't fetch on command, use the ear pinch correction.

for it, then move it so he has to stand up and walk a couple of steps to fetch it, giving occasional taps as he does these. Begin with very light taps and when these go well, move on to firmer taps in a couple of days.

With the stick in your left hand, throw the dummy a couple of feet in front of you. Do a fetch and a sit. Now add the tap of the stick with the fetch command. The sequence is: "Fetch." . . . tap . . . "Fetch" (repeating the command after the tap) . . . "Sit." Don't tap every time, but every second or third time depending on the dog's reaction. The more worried the dog, the less the taps should be used. On the first one the dog probably won't pick up the dummy. Turn around and give the fetch command again. When the dog is familiar with the more vigorous taps, you can use the ear pinch when he refuses a fetch command.

Tap the pup when you give the fetch command. Begin with a light tap, progressing to a vigorous tap.

The ideal way to practice this procedure is in a straight line. However, you may find yourself going in circles because most dogs have a tendency to go either right or left, and you're concentrating so hard you don't know where you're going. Therefore, do these sessions either on a road or a long driveway. Gradually add more distance between you and the dummy, throwing it about five to six feet out in front.

The tapping varies depending on what the dog is doing. There isn't any set schedule when to tap, when not to, how hard to tap, etc. Use your judgment here. If the dog is doing well, increase the degree of the tap. If the dog is worried, do several retrieves without taps until he's acting normally again.

To finish the stick routine, have someone walk behind you and the dog, carrying the stick. He can give an occasional tap. Continue this until the dog isn't bothered by having someone behind him. The entire stick procedure will take approximately a week. To test the results of your teaching, go really fast. Don't give the dog time to think about anything except the command you give. Watch for lunging. Don't allow him to go for the dummy until you say "Fetch." After you've done some fast fetches, do a couple of slow ones, to see if he still lunges.

Continue this exercise until the pup fetches eagerly.

Tap the pup after he dives for the dummy.

If he doesn't fetch the dummy, use the ear pinch.

FIELD WORK

Now that your pup is learning disciplined behavior in his yard work, you can expect more from him in his field work. He should walk to the line without disjointing your arm sockets. He should be sitting, with your hand on his collar, until the dummy hits the ground with no wiggling or lunging. When he returns with the dummy, give the sit command a few feet before he gets to you. Most of his sits will be in front or a little to one side. Don't insist on a return to your side yet. He will learn that in the next section of yard work.

The pup should sit while you signal for the throw. Hold the collar until the dummy is on the ground.

When your dog knows the hold, you can expect him to wait for your drop command. If he drops the dummy before the command, simply put it back in his mouth saying "Hold." Keep the marks fairly simple and uncomplicated. Your dog is learning many new things and his retrieves should be a source of relaxation for both of you.

The pup should sit in front and hold the dummy. No returning to the side yet.

7

THE BIG FINISH
CONTINUED

Yard sessions begin with two to four fun dummys or as many as needed to get him relaxed and ready to work. Include fun dummys in the middle—can the dog handle this interruption and successfully go back to work? They will conclude with fun throws to reward the dog for his effort. If your dog gets too excited when you return to work after a fun dummy, give him "business" throws. Have him sit, throw the dummy, send him on his name and have him sit on the return. This lets him have a release from the work of learning and still keeps him under control. Once a dog has been taught force fetching, he can't be allowed to drop the dummy on a fun throw. Make him fetch it up.

All training sessions should conclude with vigorous praise, to release any tension that might have developed. Each of the last three successful fetches or backs in the session should be praised with increasing enthusiasm, unless the dog really goofs and you start counting from one again. (You can't quit on a bad performance—only on three *good* ones in a row.) Each "Good dog" gets louder until the third one is a big "Okay!" with a fun dummy to let him know the session is finished and he did a good job.

The command we're teaching in this chapter is "Back," which will be used to send a dog on a blind retrieve. We begin by using "Fetch" because this is the command the dog has just learned, and it's more appropriate when the dummys are close to the dog.

During any of these sessions, if the dog can't seem to function, go back to a preceding command that the dog is familiar with and can do with success. For most dogs, we're not asking anything they're not readily capable of doing, but some dogs are lazy and don't want to learn. The high-energy dog has trouble sitting still long enough to learn.

YARDWORK

Three or four days a week is sufficient for the following section of yard work. It requires a lot of concentration and this is stressful to many pups. It doesn't matter how many weeks it takes to complete this phase. Work at each step until your pup is comfortable with it. Ideally, your pup should consistently be getting marks in the field. The field work doesn't need to be extensive—three or four marks which should now include birds.

Force to the Pile

Have your dog on-leash and stand in front of him. Three dummys will be about three feet to your right and the same on your left (more dummys will be confusing to your dog at this point). Throw a dummy to one pile and say "Fetch." Since you're teaching your dog to take one dummy off the pile, as soon as he has a dummy in his mouth say "Here" and jerk the leash. Do the same on the other side so you're working both right and left. You will know to move on to the next step when you can throw a dummy to the right, point to the left and have your dog fetch from the left pile.

Now put the dummys into one pile and move it three feet back of the pup and slightly to one side. When your dog is fetching these adequately, move the pile four to six feet behind him. Remember to have him sit facing you and return to sit facing you after each fetch command. Point to the pile each time you say "Fetch." If he refuses to fetch, say "Sit," get him under control and take the ear for an ear pinch. Then say "Fetch" again, pinch his ear, and if you did a good job with the force-fetch training, he should dive for a dummy. When you've progressed to the pile being straight behind the dog (about four to six feet) raise your arm straight up for the back command even though you're still saying "Fetch."

Always use a leash or a long line. The pup must never be able to avoid a command.

One pile is moved about halfway back.

Now the dummys are straight behind the pup.

A pup will often switch dummys when he goes to the pile. If he grabs one, spits it out and grabs another, jerk on the leash and say "Here" as soon as he picks up a dummy. If this continues to be a problem, sit him in heel position and put a pile of dummys in front. Say "Fetch," give an ear pinch, and repeat "Fetch." Make sure he picks up just one several times in succession before you move the pile behind him again.

From now on, the pile will stay a few feet behind the dog with the exception of the first two dummys that will start this drill. For these the dog will be at your side in heel position. Throw a dummy to the pile, put your hand over his head, and send him on his name. This is called "Marking the Pile" and should be done every day for quite awhile, in addition to the fun dummys thrown before training begins.

To start working on the back command (the one used for blind retrieves), sit your pup in front of you with the pile behind him. For the first few sessions, use the fetch command because he hasn't yet learned what "Back" means. Hold the leash because the dog might lunge for a dummy or he might grab more than one dummy. When he responds well to your commands, drop the leash, but keep it attached.

After the pup understands the back command, the dummys can be moved farther away.

The Slingshot

At this point the slingshot is introduced to place additional pressure on the dog. The pile of about twelve dummys is about fifteen feet from the dog. Keep it closer if your dog doesn't have a lot of stamina, or farther if he's a speedball. You'll start using your long-line now. The length should allow you to have a hold on it when the dog reaches the pile.

The first day or two, simply snap the slingshot occasionally when the dog goes to the pile (it's much easier if someone else stands behind you and works the slingshot). You say "Fetch," your helper snaps, you repeat "Fetch." Don't snap the slingshot on the next fetch. If the pup slows down or acts worried, give him several fetches without any snaps until he has regained a good attitude, then use the slingshot again. When things are going well, introduce the back command instead of fetch. However, if that creates a problem, use fetch again. You will probably go back and forth with these commands until the dog has learned what the word *back* means.

Using the Marble

When the sound of the slingshot isn't bothering the dog, start hitting him with a marble. With the dog in front, facing you, say "Fetch" or "Back" and when he has turned to go, marble his hindquarters (or the ground near his rear, depending on the aim of your helper). Always repeat the command. The sequence is: "Fetch." . . . marble . . . "Fetch." The dog might go halfway out and pop (stop and look at you). If so, say "Fetch" again (or "Back"). On the next try, say "Fetch" or "Back" again right before he gets to the place where he popped, to keep him running. Your goal during the week or two you do this drill is to get the pup used to being hit by the marble. The same procedure applies here as for the snap of the slingshot. Give a free fetch or back (no marble) after he's been marbled. Position a chair accordingly if the dog begins to flare from a straight line.

When the pup shows no negative response to being marbled close to the line, begin to marble him when he's halfway to the pile of dummys. When he shows no reaction at that distance, marble him just as he gets to the pile.

When marbled, some pups will decide not to move the next time they are sent. If this happens, go back to the ear pinch. If the pup continues to resist, take him to the pile, throw a dummy on the pile, and do the ear pinch. Gradually move back to the line, throwing more dummys at the pile and letting him retrieve each one.

Sometimes when a pup is marbled, he keeps on going beyond the pile. Using your long-line to stop his progress, give him a sit command followed by a fetch command. You might need to walk out closer to the pup and point to the pile. Use the ear pinch if necessary.

It's not uncommon for a dog to come to your left side in heel position instead of going to the pile. Pick up a dummy, position yourself halfway between the dog and the pile and throw the dummy to the pile. He might still come in to heel position. You might have to experiment with this to see what works with your pup. There aren't any standard procedures for this except to keep trying to communicate a mutual understanding with your dog.

When the back is going well, occasionally use only the voice command, with no arm signal. This tests whether he's going only on your arm movement, or on the voice command—he should respond to either.

What to Do with the Dummys

At this point, there's no need to accumulate all the dummys that your dog retrieves. Begin throwing the preceding dummy back to the pile while the pup is returning with another one. This does two things: He sees the dummy which helps his next trip to the pile but it also creates a problem because he wants to go to it immediately. You'll probably give a couple of corrections before the dog figures this out.

Now you will condition him to having dummys behind you that he must respect and leave alone. At first, toss them behind you while he's running to the pile. The next step is to place each dummy down quietly while he sits in front of you watching. Your goal is to send the pup for a dummy on the back command and have the dog come, sit, and deliver the dummy in front to you. Then say "Drop," throw it behind you, say "Back" and he will go for another dummy. Therefore, there are several things you can do with the dummy: hold on to it, get rid of it after you've sent the pup, throw it back to the pile, or maybe walk back a few feet and set it down. But if you just start throwing the dummy behind you without teaching your pup to behave, he's going to want it, which is very disrupting to the training session.

Your Pup at Your Side

With this exercise you now repeat the steps of marbling to the pile but with the pup in heel position. Your pup will have on a flat collar or a chain collar with a long-line attached, and you will hold the stick. With your pup at your left side toss a dummy to the pile. Send your pup on his name because this is a mark rather than a blind retrieve. Your pup needs to be steady for this; if not, hold his collar. When you have done this two or three times you are ready to begin.

Place your hand over his head but don't let him leave until you say "Back." About half the time, send the pup without your hand; just say "Sit" and "Back." The goal is for the dog to sit there looking at the pile. If he's doing anything else, (looking around) go ahead and send him. If he then refuses to go, use the ear pinch. Do not wait for the pup to look at the pile. This is the hardest thing for many handlers to accept—to send a pup when they *know* he's not ready, but it's the only solution. The pup must learn this for himself.

The timing for sending the pup is not always the same. When you first start doing this, the timing is an even pace—you don't want to confuse him. Once he's doing well, you should vary the timing. There are times you will say "Drop" and then send him immediately as soon as you've taken the dummy. There are times you will let him sit there a few seconds. This is done so the timing doesn't become predictable to the dog. The end result is that the dog learns to give you his undivided attention because he's doesn't know *when* you're going to say "Back."

Returning to heel position with the dummy should be done with the pup quickly lining up straight at your side. Use your stick to guide the pup's rear into a straight, quick sit at your side.

If your pup refuses to go to the pile and you're tired of the ear pinch, use your stick. Walk the pup to the pile, repeating "Back," and swatting each time with the stick. Another aid is to toss a dummy to the pile if the dog can't seem to move from your side. Throw several if necessary, sending him after each throw.

The helper gets ready before the pup is sent.

If your helper can't always be there, you can do most of the marbling now that your dog is at your side. However, the timing of the marble off the line is much better if someone else can do it. When you marble the dog halfway to the pile, and finally at the pile, everytime "Back" is said, your arm should be up in the back position to reinforce the command if the dog looks around at you.

The end result is a pup who goes and returns from the pile with enthusiasm.

Force to the Water

The pup should have had many water marks before beginning water force training. If the pup hasn't had much water opportunity, delay the water forcing until he's an eager water dog.

We hope you can find a clean piece of water narrow enough so you can keep the pup on the long-line. Forcing the pup to swim through water to get to the pile and bring back a dummy is done using the same steps that you used in marbling the pup to the pile on land. Mark the pile and let him swim for a couple of dummys first before you begin. You will start on the edge of the water with the pup sitting in front of you—as soon as he turns around and takes a step he's in the water. Marble him as soon as he is entering the water.

Use the back command with your arm straight up every time you send him. When he shows no reaction to being hit with a marble close to shore, begin to marble him about halfway across the water, and when he's confident with that, marble him just as he gets to the pile on the opposite side of the water. Use the long-line to bring your pup back into the water as soon as he has picked up a dummy from the pile on the other side. At the same time, call him, "Here!" The line is a nuisance—you have to keep pulling it in as the dog returns so pup won't get tangled. But it's the only way you can control re-entry into the water. When your pup is performing well from in front of you, repeat the procedure with him at your side in heel position. After he's been swimming to the pile a few times, throw him a fun dummy behind you on the land so he can run and warm up.

FIELD WORK

Your dog is learning advanced concepts now and needs the field work for a release of any stress he acquires during yard work, as well as for the application of yard work principles to the field, such as waiting for your command to retrieve, returning to your side, and waiting for the drop command. Make sure you give your dog at *least* as much field work as yard work, preferably more.

Now that your dog knows the hold and the fetch, you can use birds in your field work. If your dog is sitting, not lunging, and watching a dead bird be thrown, he has earned the right to have a flying bird shot for him (a "flier"). These are usually pigeons. Continue with steadying procedures here, and don't let the pup go for the bird if he lunges or even moves his front feet while you're holding the collar when the bird is shot. Make him wait until you send him.

Continue to use back-to-back singles, with either two or three gunners in the field. This helps prepare the dog for hunting conditions. As soon as the dog returns and delivers one bird, line him up facing the next gunner and signal for that one to be thrown. The length of the marks depends on the dog. If your dog is hunting wide and hard for several minutes, shorten the distance of the bird from the line. You can do this by moving up closer to where the mark will be thrown when it's your turn.

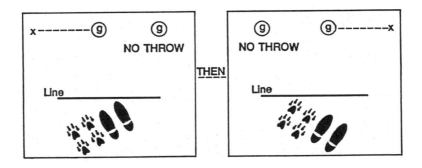

Some pups don't easily pick out the gunners. They need to be able to do this as part of learning to look out ahead and watch for a bird. Have the gunner say "Hup" for the pup (you will say "Mark,") as soon as he gets to the line. If your pup continues to have trouble looking for the gunner when he comes to the line, don't wait. Signal for the bird to be thrown. If the pup doesn't see it, signal for another bird to be thrown. This should immediately alert your pup when he comes to the line.

When your pup is marking well, not having a lot of long hunts, begin teaching him to mark the *bird*. To do this, have the gunner sit down after he throws the bird. When the pup is doing well with this situation, have the gunner lie down on the ground after he throws the bird so that he isn't visible to the pup.

Another good training experience to give the pup is to have the gunner throw the mark and as soon as the bird hits the ground, leave that position and walk to the next gunner's position, or to a nearby tree or bush. This is very distracting to the pup at first because here is someone tromping across the field, but the pup soon learns to pay attention to the bird. The gunner really has to watch the pup because at first the pup will follow the gunner. If this happens, the gunner should stop and stand still. If the pup doesn't go on hunting for the bird the handler should say "Hunt it up" or "Find it" and walk out closer to the bird, if necessary, to attract the pup over that way. As soon as the pup is going to the bird the gunner can start walking again. Most pups stop following the gunner after a few experiences. This is a valuable lesson for pups to learn because in hunting conditions, or in hunting dog stakes or a field trial where gunners retire (disappear), the dog won't become confused when gunners are moving around.

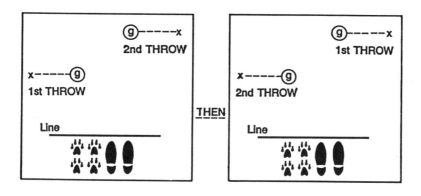

Also add variation in the positioning of the gunners. Have one long mark and one short one. Run the short mark first, then the long one. When your pup can run past the area where he has already picked up a bird and go straight to the long mark, reverse the order. Have the long one thrown first, then the short one. Another variation is to have three gunners each stand the same distance from the line;

then have two farther away and one closer; then two closer and one farther away.

With back-to-back singles and two gunners, have the birds or dummys thrown to the outside, then have one gunner throw to the outside and one to the inside, then have

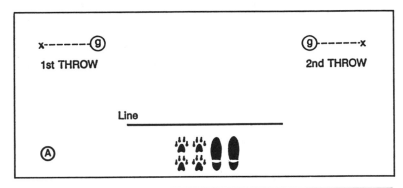

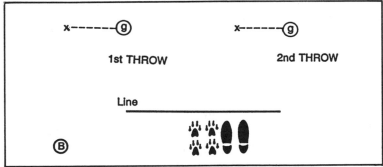

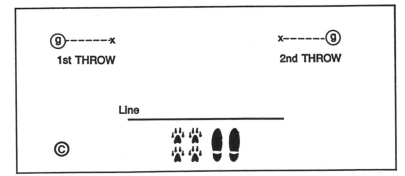

These back-to-back singles are arranged in order of difficulty, with the inside-inside throws being hardest for the pup to mark accurately.

both thrown inside (still as singles), but don't mix up these throws on the same day. When your pup is retrieving outside throws confidently, introduce one inside throw, etc.

Usually only one set of gunners will be using live guns (shooting birds), the other will be tossing dead birds and shooting blanks. Many handlers wait until the last mark to give the pup a flier because if the flier is shot on the first mark, he often won't be interested in a dead bird for his next mark, but will want to go back to the live gunners. When you progress to having multiple marks (all birds thrown before the dog begins to retrieve) the live bird often should be the first one thrown and the last one picked up.

When the pup is doing a good job of marking the fall of fliers, move the live gunner closer to the dog to simulate hunting conditions. Another way to simulate hunting conditions can be done on days when you have only one helper in the field. While the dog is returning with the bird or dummy, throw another one off to the side. Make your pup deliver his first bird to you, then send him for the other one you threw.

SUMMING UP

Expect your pup to have good manners. Walk to the line on-leash (don't let yourself be dragged). Take the leash off when you're in position at the line. Put the leash back on when you leave the line. By doing this you will be in control of your dog's behavior when he's excited. Take your stick to the line with you. Use it if your dog won't sit at your side or won't stop swinging his head. Give him a swat and repeat the sit command.

Remember to always exercise your pup before he goes to the line. Don't let him get into the habit of urinating or defecating when he's retrieving a bird. Don't let him wildly run around while he's airing; teach him to stay close. If necessary, get the slingshot and review the here command.

The well mannered hunting dog behaves both on the line and while hunting. Don't stop expecting good behavior, and one day it will be automatic. Then and only then can you relax and know you've done a good job.

GLOSSARY

Back: 1) The command used to send a dog from your side on a blind retrieve. 2) The command given to a dog who is facing you along with the straight-up arm signal to turn him running back in a straight line.

Back-To-Back-Singles: Marks that are either a double or a triple, but run as singles. As soon as the pup brings back the first bird, he watches the second mark be thrown and is sent to retrieve that one.

Blind: A retrieve in which the dog does not see the bird fall but is directed to it by arm signals and whistles.

Fall: The place where the bird/dummy falls.

Flier: Live bird released and shot.

Fun Dummy: This is play retrieving. Throw the dummy for your dog. He shouldn't sit or stay while you throw it—this is fun! He must bring the dummy back, of course, but not to a formal heel position.

Gunner: The person firing the gun. Another term for this person is "thrower" whose job it is to work with the handler, throwing the bird/dummy where the handler indicates and helping the handler in any way requested.

Line: 1) The designated place where the dog and handler stand and from where the retrieve is begun. 2) The route the dog takes to the bird/dummy.

Mark: 1) The act of watching the bird/dummy and remembering where it fell. 2) Command given to the dog to watch the bird/dummy. 3) The thrown bird/dummy. "That was a tough mark."

Marking the Pile: Showing the dog the pile of dummys before beginning training on the back command. The pup will be in heel position. throw a dummy to the pile, put your hand over his head and send him on his name.

Popping: This refers to the dog looking back to the handler for help. It can occur on a blind retrieve, or a mark, or in yard work.

Steady: When you are on the line signalling for birds to be thrown, or hunting, your dog should not move until commanded.

BIBLIOGRAPHY

BOOKS

Duffy, David Michael. (1985). *Expert Advice on Gun Dog Training* (Rev. Ed.) Piscataway, NJ: Winchester Press.

Free, James Lamb. (1980). *Training Your Retriever* (7th Rev. Ed.) New York: Putnam.

Milner, Robert. (1983). *Retriever Training for the Duck Hunter.* Princeton, NJ: Nassau Press, Inc.

Monks of New Skete. (1978). *How to be Your Dog's Best Friend.* Boston-Toronto: Little, Brown and Co.

Quinn, Tom. (1983). *The Working Retriever.* New York: E.P. Dutton, Inc.

Spencer, James B. (1983). *Retriever Training Tests.* New York: Arco Publishing, Inc.

Spencer, James B. (1988). *Hunting Retrievers: Hindsights, Foresights and Insights.* Loveland, CO: Alpine Publications, Inc.

Tortora, Daniel F. (1981). *Understanding Electronic Dog Training.* Tucson, AZ: Tri-Tronics. Inc.

Walters, D.L. & Ann Walters. (1979). *Training Retrievers to Handle.* LaCygne, KS.

PERIODICALS

Gun Dog. P.O. Box 35098, Des Moines, IA.

Retriever Field Trial News. 4213 S. Howell Ave., Milwaukee, WI 53207.

The Hunter's Whistle. American Kennel Club, 51 Madison Ave., New York, NY 10010.

Hunting Retriever, The Newsletter of the Hunting Retriever Club, Inc. (a registry for hunting breeds). United Kennel Club, 100 E. Kilgore Rd.,Kalamazoo, MI 49001.

If you would like to know more about your retriever, or about dogs in general, write for our latest FREE book catalog.

Following are some Alpine titles that may be of interest:

> *Hunting Retrievers: Hindsights, Foresights, and Insights,* by James B. Spencer.

> *Retriever Working Certificate Training,* by Branstad, Rutherford and Whicker.

> *How to Raise a Puppy You Can Live With. 2nd Ed.* by Rutherford and Neil.

> *Scent: Training to Track, Search, and Rescue,* by Pearsall and Verbruggen.

> *Practical Scent Training,* by Lue Button.

> *Canine Hip Dysplasia and other Orthopedic Diseases,* by Fred Lanting.

Your comments and suggestions on *Retriever Puppy Training* are also welcomed.

Alpine Publications
P. O. Box 7027
Loveland, CO 80537

Call Toll Free 1-800-777-7257